ESOTERIKA

Also by Mitch Horowitz

Practical Magick
Modern Occultism
Occult America
One Simple Idea
The Miracle Club
Uncertain Places
Daydream Believer
The Seeker's Guide to the Secret Teachings of All Ages
The Miracle Habits
The Miracle Month
The Power of the Master Mind
Magician of the Beautiful
Mind As Builder
Cosmic Habit Force
Happy Warriors
The Miracle of a Definite Chief Aim
Secrets of Self-Mastery
Awakened Mind
The 30-Day Mental Challenge
The Sixth Sense

ESOTERIKA

FORMULAS AGAINST THE FALSE SELF

MITCH HOROWITZ

Published 2026 by Gildan Media LLC
aka G&D Media
www.GandDmedia.com

Front cover design by Tom McKeveny

Interior design by Meghan Day Healey of Story Horse, LLC.

Library of Congress Cataloging-in-Publication Data is available upon request

ISBN: 978-1-7225-0762-6

10 9 8 7 6 5 4 3 2 1

"He travels the fastest who travels alone."

Contents

INTRODUCTION

Esoterika

Every generation believes it lives on a precipice. That is near-universal. Historically, our era differs little from most in its apocalyptic expectancy. But a different and, in my view, more pernicious spectre haunts our age.

It is the nearly global attitude that we are living an *unreal existence*: blinded by artifice, strangers to ourselves, and acclimated to ersatz reality.

Our alienation, broadly gnostic—echoing the late-ancient sects who rejected the material world as the simulation of a false deity—plots our most popular movies, books, television shows, and video games; this media resonates with international audiences across disparate cultures. Simulation theory haunts us. *The Matrix* is our Beatles.

If there is one thing that everyone can seem to agree on: we are not ourselves. This sensation is correct.

The pangs of doubt we feel toward ourselves and our surroundings are responses to the automaticity of our existence. We traverse life with a menu of, say, twenty responses, and claim selfhood. That is not real existence. Neither we nor others around us are functioning as beings supposedly made in the image of a creator or as the likely older Hermetic dictum goes: *as above, so below.*

In Western culture, our unease is compounded by loss of civility, technological displacement, and directionless prosperity, which are producing a generation of ennui, rage, and despair. To that, I have no macro solutions. But I do have formulas that expose the narrowness of our being—our *false being*—and that, frankly, take a goddamn hammer to what keeps us there. Along with that hammer come a lot of ideals and high wishes for your happiness.

The hour is late. It is time for unwanted guests to leave.

My title word *esoterika* is, like *magick*, a purposeful rupture with common usage. Beneath its banner, I join esoteric (inner) and occult (hidden) teachings not only in exposition but direct application to your immediate life.

To achieve this, *Esoterika* brings unseen philosophy into explicitness and practicality. Viewed traditionally, my effort reflects a downward octave. Or, in exoteric terms, entropy. The stress and digitized hyper-stimulus of current life demands it. In any case, descent is lawful; damning it is damning the seasons.

The "false self" referenced in my subtitle is, in part, the product of conformity, a force from which none of us is ever free. For the grounded individual seeking greater self-agency, fuller personal expression, and—not quite *freedom*, a jejune and impractically distant ideal given the forces, metaphysical and physical, arrayed against us—but rather *dignity within circumstance*, some modicum of accelerant is needed. A hammer, too, is needed. This book is it.

Our present age requires a *philosophy of results*. What good is amassing knowledge, customary or symbolic, when such things fail to penetrate and transform? It is the equivalent of reading—or worse, reciting—a recipe to sate hunger. *Esoterika* is no recipe book. It fosters self-development. The book's "formulas against the false self" are necessarily incomplete but potent. A *formula* is a concise expression within the sciences. That intent animates my effort.

* * *

The ideas in this book emerge from rejected or discontinued threads of Western esotericism and occult philosophy. Obscurity has, for now, spared these esoteric insights from dilution and reification.

I reconstitute neglected fragments in *Esoterika* from Hermetic (Greek-Egyptian), pre- or early Abrahamic (Judaic-Christian-Sufi), and modern esoteric traditions, and wed them to my own lived experience, which is, I warrant, yours too—as no life is exclusive.

Everything in this book is something to try. Not everything in this book is an outlook to share; if I wanted your agreement I would write a polemic. I want your *understanding* that tools of the psyche—an amalgam of intellect and emotion—are greater than we know, and that religious-philosophical history, as a container of such tools, reaches us through conditioned acceptancy, which several of my historical references and chapters work to interrogate.

My effort is, in a sense, schismatic. It reflects no single thought school. Philosophically, it is a mutt. But, as verified through your use, these formulas directly address, and leaven, our present predicament. As such, a particular potency resides in these chapters. Their ideas, if practiced seriously, will change you in positive ways. You will be more agentic, expressive, and, hence, happier. For the determined, this change occurs quickly.

I mean this so fully that chapter one offers, at some authorial risk, a chin-out exercise in wishing. It is the snake in the garden.

* * *

Some pedants debate the nature of "real philosophy." It is like debating real medicine. If a method proves therapeutic, it is *real* in the sense of soundness, verity, and relevance.

I see no other principles worthy of your search.

In that vein, personal philosophy must be measured in the conduct and experience of the seeker. This ideal dwells in the thought and soundest interpretations of Hegel, Nietzsche, Emerson, and the mystical and classical masters of antiquity, from the Vedic families of India to Confucius to Plato.

Since relatively early in the modern revival of the search for ancient spiritual origins during the Renaissance—by spiritual, I mean extraphysical—the outlook I embrace has been grouped under the English term *occult* from Latin *occultus* for secret or hidden. Within Renaissance culture, *occult* labeled rediscovered shards, sometimes posthumously reconstructed, of interrupted religious ideas from Egypt, Greece, Rome, and Persia. The central idea of occultism, conceptually simple yet implicitly seismic, is the existence of unseen dimensions or intersections of time, all possessed of their own events, causes, intelligences, and perhaps iterations of ourselves; the influence of these realms is felt on and through us without mediation by religion or congregation.

In strict terms, occultism is a Western concept. There exist esoteric (from Greek *esoterikós* for inner) teachings within Vedic, Buddhist, Animist, Taoist, Confucian, and Shamanic traditions around the world—but occultism emerged from the West's rupture with its religious roots during the rise of the Abrahamic religions, particularly early Christendom as distinct from the philosophy of Christ.

In an important demarcation, occultism differs from esotericism. The esoteric usually corresponds to an exoteric or outer counterpart, generally a traditional religion of which esotericism reflects the inner core. The occult is independent of religion—though not necessarily rejecting of it. My term *esoterika* unites both occultism and esotericism in application and immediacy.

I use another term, already referenced: *magick*. British artist and occultist Aleister Crowley (1875–1947) revived the early modern English spelling to distinguish it from stagecraft. His effort inspires mine. I define magick as *causative ritual*. It is perhaps the razor's edge of philosophical application. Magickal agencies, whether metaphysical, psychological, or some combination, are ponderable. Their worth, like everything offered here, is measured in impact on the individual. Anything else is a matter of taste.

Lamplights

Most mainstream intellects and pedagogues consider occultism—when they do at all—as gimmick or superstition. Frankfurt School philosopher Theodor W. Adorno wrote in his essay "Theses Against Occultism" in 1947: "Occultism is the metaphysic of dunces."

He was wrong. I evince his error. Yet Adorno's guild-view helped me realize that many of the intellectuals I admired growing up were susceptible to judging *category of query versus scale of quality*, or topic over treatment. That is the barstool next to ersatz seriousness. Overused, it leads to dowdiness and foolishness.

We are all generalists—there is no escaping that. But using general knowledge to determine what to study and why invites oversight. *Worse still, some scholars omit such lines of inquiry altogether.* Distinguished historians and biographers often neglect occult-influenced episodes and relationships—sometimes of a pivotal nature—in the lives of their subjects, including Frederick Douglass (hoodoo), Mahatma Gandhi (Theosophy), Charles Lindbergh (Spiritualism), Theodore Dreiser (paranormalism), and Upton Sinclair (telepathy).

Having stated that, I wish to note my positive influences. Several names recur throughout in this book but here I reference some who may not appear explicitly. They undergird my effort without necessarily sharing my viewpoint. One is British historian Frances Yates (1899–1981) who wrote several pioneering books about the influence of occultism, Hermeticism, alchemy, and Kabbalah in early modern life.

Her work roused academic letters to at least fitfully acknowledge the impact, intellectually and historically, of occult thought, which most historians had, due to cultural affinity with philosophical materialism—and reasons little deeper—conscripted to obscurity and frivolity.

The Occult Philosophy in the Elizabethan Age, published in 1979, was Yates's last full-length book before her death in 1981. Discovering it at a transition in my early thirties, I found the work revealing, meticulous, and resonant with the basic but neglected question: *what have we missed?* That query saves ships from sinking—and intellects, both individually and generationally, from ossifying.

Occultism, as Yates saw it, is a modern reclaiming of the Egyptian-Greek-Roman-Persian fragments of mystical and Hermetic philosophy, infused into ancient philosophy and pedantry, but often lost in particulars. The central Hermetic idea is psyche as medium to greater dimensions and, hence, instrument of spiritual expansion. Although it exceeds my scope here, I must add that Hermeticism as a philosophy has reached us in pieces. Of the *Corpus Hermeticum*, the Renaissance-era translation of late-ancient philosophical tracts, we possess no originals, neither Alexandrian, Byzantine, nor Florentine. Intervening centuries have produced varying—and necessarily subjective—translations and textual shuffling. I consider this theme further in chapter ten.

The Renaissance and early Enlightenment, including the triumph of heliocentricity, liberal query, Romanticism, and developing fields of modern medicine, engineering, and chemistry bear indelible markings of occult revivalism, Christianized Kabbalah, alchemy, Hermeticism, and Freemasonry, arguably the final outpost of Renaissance occultism. Early Masonic lights appear among key founders of the British Royal Society, a bastion of Enlightenment thought.

I discovered esoteric Egyptologist R. A. Schwaller de Lubicz (1887–1961) through the memoir *Al-Kemi: Hermetic, Occult, Political, and Private Dimensions of R.A. Schwaller de Lubicz* by André VandenBroeck. I encountered this work of esoteric intrigue in 2005 on the brink of my authorial career. It fortified my conviction that occultism is, at its subtlest, not only intellectually sound, but thrilling.

The 1987 portrait of Schwaller evokes strange memories filled with vulnerability. Its mysterious author, VandenBroeck, was then living in retirement at a hotel in Mexico managed by his son. His publisher gave me his fax number. "I do not participate in the internet," VandenBroeck wrote me. He sent a friendly fax in response to my initial outreach noting that he used to live on New York's Hudson Street where my publishing company then sat. Thereafter he went silent. I had the impression, perhaps retrocausal in nature, that he did not wish me to write an expository appreciation of his book. His publisher, too, previously friendly, went silent.

My path is not theirs. It is one of exposition. Ancient logic is splitting one to get two. Modern logic is adding one to get two. Exposition is not *l'expérience* (which can also mean experiment) but, as Schwaller observed, it is next best.

"The reason for this lack of contact," André wrote in *Al-Kemi*, "holds no mystery: he [Schwaller] did not believe in language. Yet it is through language, both his and mine, that I discovered him."

My work, in its practical vein, attempts—with clinical data (very modern)—to elucidate the language of Schwaller's ineffable truth of time as "spherical spiral" versus progressing line. It is my effort to drag the ineffable into what literary critic Irving Howe—another intellectual hero growing up—in his 1986 *The American Newness* called "the shallows of the explicit." That is the job I have assumed. It was open and I accepted it.

* * *

These were not my only influences. They also include the writing of Richard Smoley—in particular, his 1997 essay "Masonic Civilization." It first ran in the Alexandrian-scale journal *Gnosis*.

Richard demonstrated, in sparkling prose and thought, how esoteric questions of true impact lie just beneath the floorboards of outer life, including enduring Masonic influence on American framings of free speech and protection of the search for meaning.

A later influence arrived in the work of artist and author Carl Abrahamsson, who demonstrated a depth of thought in Satanic, Thelemic, and Lefthand paths that I had not previously sensed.

I am also shaped by the writing and philosophy of Jacob Needleman (1934–2022), who I published for years. His work elevates the capacity to sustain doubt. Ex nihilo certainties kill the search. Intellectually, if not personally, Jerry, as friends knew him, displayed no such resting points. He titled one of his essay anthologies, now unavailable, *The Indestructible Question*. I embrace that principle. It is the only measure—*sincerity of question*—by which I choose colleagues.

I had literary heroes from my youth—most of whom would have proven indifferent if not averse toward the topics I later embraced—including the aforementioned Irving Howe (1920–1993). Following Irving's memorial service, the widow of socialist philosopher-activist Michael Harrington—another influence, who we lost too soon in 1989—took my hands and said: "Mitch, *standards*. If you want to learn one thing from Irving, that's it. *Standards*."

Through these figures, to which I add scholar of religion Jeffrey J. Kripal and historian Joscelyn Godwin, I also detect intimate linkage between *posterity and generosity*. Without generosity—of thought, query, and character—vines of influence wither. Greatness of intellect cannot exist without generosity. Be careful how you read that. In the search, generosity is not indulgence but exchange.

Anonymous figures, one in particular, appear throughout this book. I withhold names due to veneration. I wish to suggest no association to my credit undeserved.

"Spiritual Means Truthful"

One of the chief barriers to the search is recitative wisdom, i.e., that which we glean from translations of translations of classical and ancient literature, which we then repeat to ourselves and others so often that certain concepts appear intrinsically true. Hence, they form premises from which to search. This usually dictates outcome, if any occurs.

Presently, my search is dedicated to seeking pre-consensus or primeval ideas in ancient religion and ethics—again, they reach us fragmentarily—before such things grew codified and conditioned.

In that framing, an interesting topic is *anger.* Across the traditions, as they endure, anger is understood, I assume rightly, as destructive. But there exist contrary perspectives.

In the Vedic guide to civil conduct, *Arthashastra* (earliest form fourth century B.C.), the semi-legendary sage Bháradvája, who lived before recorded time, is attributed with a dissenting statement about the destructiveness of anger:

> No, says Bháradvája, anger is the characteristic of a righteous man. It is the foundation of bravery; it puts an end to despicable (persons); and it keeps the people under fear. Anger is always a necessary quality for the prevention of sin. (1915 translation by R. Shamasastry)

David Lynch told me in a 2016 interview: "This thing of righteous anger is fine, you can be against something, really truly against something, and fight for something you believe in. You'll have more energy to do that. You'll have more power, more edge to really get in and get the thing the way you want it." He said this in reference to Transcendental Meditation, a practice I share.

Do not rush heterodox ideas into hasty application. Do not embrace them without context. Even Bháradvája's brief statement contains several folds. I offer this digression because I wish to signal that dissenting ideas populate this book. My dissents may interest readers who wonder, as I once did, what the path offers those of us disappointed with the main roads.

Writing from off the main roads, I have, at times, asked whether in truth's service I am negative. There is a hardness to this book. It is in the form of calluses. In his 1919 disruption of materialist science, *The Book of the Damned*, Charles Fort (1874–1932), whose full dimensions philosophically have not yet been understood (outside scholar Jason Reza Jorjani) writes: "Our acceptance is that Evil is the negative state, by which we mean the state of maladjustment, discord, ugliness, disorganization, inconsistency, injustice, and so on . . ." You will find none of that in *Esoterika*. You will find astringency—with ideals. You will also find validation of something else David Lynch said: "Spiritual, I guess, means truthful."

ONE

Wish Come True?

My metaphysics are for the people. And they work.

I take seriously the pressures you face. I take seriously, too, the manner in which our religious and therapeutic cultures often attempt—wrongly, in most cases—to redefine the individual's questions, needs, and strivings.

I consider the mature, sensitive individual wholly capable of identifying and defending his or her private conceptions of happiness.

If there is one principle to my philosophy, one core idea underlying this book, it is this: a hungry person needs not a statement on food—but food.

In Scripture and esoteric teaching, *food is transmission*.

As promised, I offer something you can consume right now. I do not provide the metaphysical theory behind why it works. That framework is folded within this book and considered explicitly in some of my others.

That this formula *does work* is subject to your purview. Prove me right or wrong. I state that with ease.

If you like, call what you are about to encounter a trick. Sometimes a trick works. This is one such time.

1. In a period of privacy, ask yourself—without embarrassment or self-censorship—what you really, truly want. It can be intimate, material, situational—anything. Be sure your emotions are innerly expressed in earnest. *Emotional sincerity is vital.* Damn all internalized peer pressure or "spiritual" ideals. Be vulnerable. Be stark.
2. When forming your wish, never confuse or conflate means with ends. You do not necessarily need to focus on a single solution—or on any solution. Things reach you by many roads. Do not hem yourself in with mind's-eye limits or channels.
3. Hold your wish. Speak it aloud to self. If you are alone, in nature, or on a platform as a train arrives, shout it.
4. Write it down on a slip of paper or index card. Wrap it in clear packing tape to protect it and place it in your pocket. Carry it like a talisman. The very act clarifies. It also creates something in nascence that was not previously present.
5. Run your wish through your mind as often as possible. Do this with emotion as though you are an actor rehearsing a part.

6. Pray for your wish to whatever Greater Force you seek relations with, if any. If none, appeal to infinite matter or chaos.
7. Recite your wish as you drift to sleep, i.e., in the highly suggestible, mentally subtle state of hypnagogia. Repeat this upon awakening.
8. Tell absolutely no one what you are doing. We confide problems to dilute them. Talk dissipates, silence concentrates.
9. Record what happens. *Try.*

Be Careful?

People sometimes invoke the hoary but reasonable caution: *Be careful what you wish for; you just might get it.*

Sounded throughout fables, this maxim has myriad iterations. Its modern roots appear in Johann Wolfgang von Goethe (1749–1832), later popularized conceptually by Ralph Waldo Emerson (1802–1882). With a nod to Goethe's *Faust*, Emerson wrote in his 1860 essay "Fate":

> And the moral is that what we seek we shall find; what we flee from flees from us; as Goethe said, "what we wish for in youth, comes in heaps on us in old age," too often cursed with the granting of

> our prayer: and hence the high caution, that, since we are sure of having what we wish, we must beware to ask only for high things.

I am smitten with this popular—and shrewdly simple—sounding by American short-story writer Sarah Orne Jewett (1849–1909) from her 1894 *Betty Leicester's Christmas*:

> In Tideshead that summer Betty Leicester learned two things which she could not understand quite well enough to believe at first, but which always seem more and more sensible to one as time goes on. The first is that you must be careful what you wish for, because if you wish hard enough you are pretty sure to get it; and the second is, that no two persons can be placed anywhere where one will not be host and the other guest. One will be in position to give and to help and to show; the other must be the one who depends and receives.

Now do you see why I value the literature of popular metaphysics? Mysterious wisdom is etched within this neglected stone.

I cannot deny the possibility of a wish arriving via unhappy channels.

I also cannot deny the agony of a lifetime with a wish denied.

In frankness, I have conditioned some wishes. For example, in matters of success I am not interested in exploitation, sensationalism, or tragedy, visited on self or another. To protect my values, I have enunciated certain wishes narrowly.

But—stipulations slow arrival. Nature works through the quickest and most established channels available. A fire is the fastest means of clearing brush. *As above, so below.* The more you proscribe arrival, the more circuitous it will prove.

Be haunted by Rudyard Kipling's 1888 poem "The Winners":

Down to Gehenna, or up to the Throne,
He travels the fastest who travels alone.

Do you want your wish badly enough to allow it to stand alone?

I issue no admonitions one way or another. If you say, "I cannot live without . . ."—and you are wholly honest—then that urgency may be your guide.

People sometimes ask about eros and wishes: can you wish for the love of another? You can wish for anything you want—and you will do so with or without my approbation, especially in matters of romance, where logic is never at the table.

Here I return to the deceptive simplicity of Sarah Orne Jewett: "no two persons can be placed anywhere where one will not be host and the other guest." Entire lives are wrecked by failure to glean her young heroine's insight. Know your place. Understand your relationships. Two objects in magnetic pull cannot be separated any more than two in opposition can be joined.

Even if *the world is as you are*—which I firmly believe—love obeys its own law. It is the channel of life recreating itself. Its currents are upstream from our powers. Eros is transmutable in the individual—but in matters of two, it abides by different laws.

Once I was in a romance that was driving me into distraction and confusion. What other kind is there? I asked a friend for advice. He replied, "Nothing about love makes sense so just go ahead and throw yourself into it." He was, of course, right; and I would have been pulled down that path regardless: passion owns us, not us it.

One thing I am certain of: power arises from concentration on a single point. One absolute wish—sincere, private, and focused—can become that point of concentration, across all facets of life, physically, emotionally, intellectually, and metaphysically.

You can, I suspect, feel the truth of this possibility, just as in the statement by Sarah's "Sister Betty."

That is why I emphasize stark honesty in enunciating your wish. Emotions never lie. We run on them. They sustain your wish. The deeper the well you dig, the surer you are of good water. Dig deeply.

Postscript: *Try*

You will note that several times in this book, I use the term *Try*. It is my personal motto, adopted from pioneering modern occultist and self-invented mage P.B. Randolph (1825–1875).

In his book *Dealings with the Dead*, written in 1861 or 1862, Randolph wrote that an unseen intelligence named Thotmor told him: "Our motto—the motto of the greater order of which I was a brother on earth,—an order which has, under a variety of names, existed since the very dawn of civilization on the earth is 'Try'."

The seeker claimed it as his slogan. He further defined the principle "Try" through his term *Volantia* in his 1874 book *Eulis!*: "the quiet, steady, calm, non-turbulent, non-muscular exertion of the human Will."

This is sometimes rendered alternately, possibly through elaboration of another writer:

> It is simply a quiet power, and requires no muscular or nervous, but simply a still, mental force, to urge it into play, when it is feeble, as in most it is; it should be cultivated by thinking determinedly, at intervals, of one thing only at a time to the total exclusion of every thing, topic, or subject besides.

I encourage parallel study of the book *Meetings with Remarkable Men* by G.I. Gurdjieff (1866–1949) in which the twentieth-century teacher references "the law-conformable result of a man's unflinching perseverance in bringing all his manifestations into accordance with the principles he has consciously set himself in life for the attainment of a definite aim."

Randolph's motto, *Try*, echoes the simple command issued to the hero of the *Bhagavad Gita*: "Fight, Arjuna."

TWO

"Good Things Always Arrive Unexpectedly"

You possess greater solutions than you know. Not consolation-prize solutions of unbidden insight—but tactile things and conditions.

"What do you do when someone offers you a gift?" Jacob Needleman asked me.

I stared at him blankly. He replied, "You accept it!"

We routinely reject remarkable gifts. We do so because we fail to recognize them as such.

Our resistance to unexpected forms of help—cleaving to the self's narrow image of what should save it—obfuscates mysterious channels through which flow solutions, remedies, and rescues.

Solutions and endowments usually violate your mind's-eye image of what is right or suited to you.

Prejudices undermine help. *When a thing works, use it.*

This lesson, tucked into esoteric traditions, may unlock where you wish to go in life. Or where you must.

It is the Law of Solutions. This law is not a simple cause and effect but a contextual relation to life, seen and unseen. This chapter explores its dimensions.

Cast Out

I begin with a personal story about a solution I might have shunned.

In 1997, I was fired (the first of two times) from my "dream job" as an editor at a political imprint at Simon & Schuster. I had worked there only two years and my failure came as a crushing disappointment.

Seeking new work, I interviewed with some of the most prominent figures in New York City letters. All signs were promising. But—no offers emerged. I lived from paycheck-to-paycheck and urgently needed work. I found it when I was offered a lateral move to a somewhat backwater, struggling New Age publisher.

I believe in walking through open doors. The new job was a drastic stepdown in prestige. Old friends and contacts abandoned me. Senior colleagues insulted me. But rather than use my reduced position as a springboard to a more august one, I determined to stay put. I found myself attracted to a wide array of metaphysical works on the backlist, not only reawakening childhood interests but eventually rediscovering myself as a writer.

"You are the best-kept secret at this company," my boss told me. Not exactly. I was not seeking corporate recognition. I was after what I eventually found: thought leadership and authorial prominence. I discovered that I could contribute intellectual gravitas to a New Age and alternative-spiritual culture in desperate need of it.

This fulfills a maxim from the Talmudic digest *Pirkei Avos* ("Ethics of the Fathers"): "In a place where there are no men, strive to be a man." (2:6 Hebrew Publishing Company, 1949)

Had I rejected my life preserver in favor of something reputationally better, or cut ties as soon as that something appeared, you would not be reading these words right now.

It is often said that everything happens for a reason. I doubt that. But symmetry appears—or is lost—in how we regard solutions.

Be Flexible

Solutions flee custom or misplaced principle. Here are two such cases, both health related, although broadly applicable. One is grave.

At the press where I landed, we issued a popular book on holistic cures for sinus infections, a chronic problem for millions of people. At one point, the author himself contracted a painful sinus infection. He could not shake it. He "wrote the book"—literally in this case—on natural treatments. But this time they failed him.

He took an antibiotic. He recovered. I appreciated his candor in telling me. He abandoned neither principle nor program. Rather, he released closed-circuit consistency for breadth of effort. Solutions often require sacrificing something. (That is why hyper-partisans or fanatics rarely fix anything.)

I relate another episode, roughly contemporaneous, and deeply tragic. I write it from firsthand knowledge. I ask that you seek no viewpoint in it beyond my stated aim in this chapter. There is none. A good man trained as a homeopath. He suffered an infection following oral surgery. He rejected or delayed the pharmacological course described above. The result was a disabling stroke.

Subculture pressure, guild mentality, or "what worked before," can present the chief barrier to solutions. When in need, be exquisitely flexible.

Metaphysical Principles

I am influenced by the radical idealism of mystic Neville Goddard (1905–1972). Neville taught that reality consists of your emotionalized thoughts and mental pictures pushed out into the world, actually and completely. He argued for this extreme thesis with elegant simplicity and personal aplomb.

Let us, for a moment, suspend debate over Neville's point of view. Let us assume its verity. None of what Neville says contradicts my point in this chapter. Receiving what works, versus mirrors expectation, carries into the metaphysical realm. Solutions generally reach us through *the most direct and established channels available.* Such channels may drastically diverge from your preferences. That is why Neville said to watch for a "bridge of incident"—but not dictate it.

A new job does not just appear—it comes through a friend, referral, or, sometimes, a remarkable act of kismet. Other times—though infrequently—it arrives through merit. Do you damn the bridge that led you to the door of gainful employment?

A friend is a minister in Religious Science or Science of Mind, the religious-idealist movement founded by Ernest Holmes (1887–1960), and now neutered into Centers for Spiritual Living. Ernest, a lovely man, enunciated an outlook similar to Neville's. My colleague said something I always admired: "A solution can appear in a little pill as much as in any other path of creation."

Idealism, the philosophy of perceptual reality, does not hinge on forms.

Established Channels

Among ways we neglect solutions is dismissing them as too mundane. We overlook enormous gifts in this way.

Due to the framework of life, there exists likelihood that your intention will arrive through established channels, i.e., seemingly common or pedestrian (hence easily missed) points of arrival.

Socialist activist and New Thought pioneer Wallace D. Wattles (1860–1911) in his shrewd effort of applied idealism, 1910's *The Science of Getting Rich*, observed:

> In creating, the Formless seems to move according to the lines of motion it has established; the thought of an oak tree does not cause the instant formation of a fullgrown tree, but does start in motion the forces which will produce the tree, along established lines of growth.
>
> Every thought of form, held in thinking Substance, causes the creation of the form, but always, or at least generally, along lines of growth and action already established.
>
> The thought of a house of a certain construction, if it were impressed upon Formless Substance, might not cause the instant formation of the house; but it would cause the turning of creative energies

> already working in trade and commerce into such channels as to result in the speedy building of the house. And if there were no existing channels through which the creative energy could work, then the house would be formed directly from primal substance without waiting for the slow processes of the organic and inorganic world.

The principle of working along established lines is one of the subtlest in practical spirituality. Some who use spellwork or ceremonial magick take this principle a step further. When prescribing a spell or ceremony—which is ritualized intention, no different from Wattles' formula for "thinking in a Certain Way"—they note that for such operations to succeed, there must exist means of arrival.

For example, if you wish for companionship but resist company—or resist intelligent capitulations to improving personal appeal—there is no evident channel of delivery. But if you wish for companionship and actively attempt these things, you provide corresponding means of fulfillment. Magick complements muscular effort. Neither replaces the other.

Each individual must consider this step privately. Are you asking for something that fits the context of your life, practices, values, and habits? Do there exist foreseeable means of delivery?

Relatedly, are you neglecting or overlooking patterns of fulfillment—and perhaps arrival of what you need because it presents in unfamiliar ways? Allow yourself freedom in this regard. Focus on the condition you wish to attain—not the limited, mind's-eye form of attainment.

Reject nothing out of hand.

Embarrassing Episode

Your private conception of selfhood harbors solutions. Let no one dictate it to you.

In this vein, I share a story that appears in *The Miracle Club*. When I was a child, the rabbi of our local synagogue in Bellerose, Queens, started wearing a toupee. Some judged him for it, arguing that a spiritual leader should model self-acceptance and teach that life's highest values are unseen. (I frame this more gracefully than it was stated on 251st Street, but that was the general gist.)

My older sister, in a crushingly embarrassing moment, confronted him over it one Saturday morning on a greeting line after services.

"Don't you think that's a little ridiculous?" she said.

"I don't think that's any of your affair," he replied through tight lips.

I was mortified. I remain so writing these words. The rabbi was correct—not just about the confrontation but also about his choice. His detractors were wrong.

I am adamant that there is absolutely nothing wrong with pursuit of beauty, as you conceive it, and with reforming overt circumstances, including physicality, to your image of the good. Beauty as a culturally conditioned, though sometimes innate, model appears across every culture in history. I do not see its cultivation as ethically fraught. Ethics, i.e., reciprocity, describe method—not outcome.

Personal solutions can—and almost must—meet us in ways not typically sanctioned in our subgroups, including alternative or traditional spiritual cultures. Otherwise you would not need solutions—they would be in front of you. I am going to name some solutions. Some readers will not like them. That is inevitable. They include cosmetic surgery, pharmaceuticals, A.I., sex appeal, fashion, fitness, salesmanship, and social connections. I hate the last, having grown up with none. But I cannot omit it.

Note that at the top of the last paragraph, I wrote *solutions*—not *development*.

The two may coincide. This usually occurs in matters of self-expression. But they differ. Both are necessary. Neither transcends the other. You live in the world. Its demands are felt. You can refine your response to those demands. But do not get carried away or distracted. An effective life, worthy of the term, must bend to both pragmatism and principle. Remember the pill maxim.

That stated, I disdain fraud and insincerity. I disdain buying followers on social media or concealing paid endorsements (things I never do). I am sickened by our cheap habits of selling a thing by persuading people it is already selling. Or fomenting FOMO (fear of missing out). Or treating "likes" on social media as currency. Beneath all these is *seeking prestige through denunciation.* If you deplore a person or idea, surpass it.

Honor Favors

I believe that lives are twisted into torment because of solutions rejected. Or generosity withheld. They are intimately linked.

When I was ten years old, adult cousins asked my parents a special favor. They were moving into our Queens school district—but would get settled too late for their daughter, my age, to start elementary school that fall. Wishing to avoid the girl entering her new school in January—with obvious social unease—they asked to register her as a resident of our address. She would not move in but use our address to enroll.

My parents refused. Not for any reason of substance. They just did not feel like extending themselves. I was ashamed.

Trouble soon followed them . . . and followed. In my birth family, meanness and stinginess were the general rule. I am certain that when they refused to passively help a ten-year-old girl transition to a new school, they set a path for themselves.

Withholding repels solutions.

This truth is coded into religious and mythical parables across time and tradition. In what follows, indulge a historical exegesis. It pays you dividends.

"Entertain Strangers"

Religion and myth abound with parables of a god, genie, or transcendent messenger disguised as a wandering stranger. Most shun him. Those who shelter him are showered with favors. This whispers a secret about solutions.

"Be not forgetful to entertain strangers," reads Hebrews 13:2 (KJV), "for thereby some have entertained angels unawares." This references Abraham and Sarah welcoming three wanderers unveiled as angels (rooted in Greek "messengers"). Seen esoterically, strangers are solutions.

My teacher experienced friction with people who resented what they considered his overbearing style. And yet . . . he sometimes brought back into the fold a truly obnoxious yet fitfully brilliant architect who had been cast out and formed an esoteric group of his own. Why, I wondered, were we spending occasional weekends with this bombastic man?

Someone who had argued with my teacher said, "Jon does not crucify people."

The stranger or vagabond—a lone and vulnerable traveler—was considered under sacred protection in Hellenic religion, as was the fratricidal Cain in ancient Judaism. Remember this next time you shun someone.

As a rule, group shunnings stand on unsound foundations—or rot existing ones. Groups that expel people soon fray. This includes friend groups.

In *The Odyssey* (Book IX), Odysseus declares:

> [We] have come as suppliants to thy knees, in the hope that thou wilt give us entertainment, or in other wise make some present, as is the due of strangers. Nay, mightiest one, reverence the gods; we are thy suppliants; and Zeus is the avenger of suppliants and strangers—Zeus, the strangers' god—who ever

> attends upon reverend strangers. (translated by A.T. Murray, Loeb Classical Library, 1919)

The wanderer is not only watched over—but gods themselves assume such forms, walking among us unknown. In *Works and Days* (c. 700 B.C.), poet Hesiod cautions:

> For the eye of Zeus, seeing all things and understanding all things, is upon us. If he will, he sees straightway what justice is this city's, what violence. For the immortals are ever about the cities, and with them is Zeus who watches over men's violence and justice. (adapted from Hugh G. Evelyn-White, Loeb Classical Library, 1914)

In *Metamorphoses*, Ovid (43 B.C.–c. 17/18 A.D.) recounts Jupiter (Zeus) and Mercury (Hermes) disguising themselves as vagabonds to test mortal hospitality. They are repeatedly rejected until fed and sheltered by a poor elderly couple—who are rewarded with immortality, transformed at death into sacred trees, while the corrupt region around them is destroyed.

Persian Sufi master Rumi (1207–1273) expressed the same ethic: "Every guest that cometh to thee is a messenger sent from the Unseen; receive him well . . ." (adapted from *The Mathnawí of Jalálu'ddín Rúmí*, vol. II, translated by Reynold A. Nicholson, Cambridge University Press, 1926)

My teacher witnessed a student of spiritual philosopher G.I. Gurdjieff—French journalist, photographer, and writer René Zuber (1902–1979), author of *Who Are You, Monsieur Gurdjieff?* (1954)—abide a traditional Sufi oblation or *zikr* ("remembrance of God"). Zuber prepared a pot of soup and spent the whole day waiting by a roadside for a traveler upon whom to bestow it.

In classical thought, hospitality, a lost or under-appreciated ancient code, proves a harbinger of solutions. Within this sits the subtler message that solutions, like gods, arrive unannounced or undetected.

* * *

I offer two stories in rejecting hierarchical or mob judgments, which deter solutions.

I made a vow in 2017: I will not curse the outsider.

I do not reference the outsider as sanitized in museum cases, comfortably distant history, or academic-literary theory.

I mean the outsider extant in cultural currency.

That is why I correspond with inmates. A few of whom, it should be said, may be innocent. Most are not.

I do this because I know how it feels to be judged.

Years ago in my corporate publishing days I knew a copy editor whom I could not stand. Her work was obsessive rather than meticulous. It placed needless burdens on writers who had already done a good job. In one instance I refused—flat out—to send her queries to an able historian. His work was done.

Random House took over our company. This was sold to staff, media, and the public as a merger. That was false. The new bosses began firing people. This copy editor went first. (They took four years to get to me.) The moment I heard, my eyes welled with tears. I made a beeline to her office to express solidarity. She was already gone.

A colleague is a clinical professor of psychiatry at Georgetown. He recounted to me witnessing people abandon figures who had lost authority, like deposed department heads. He described such personal abandonment as "disgusting."

When I was fired for the second and last time from publishing, someone to whom I had lent collegial and material help—in concrete terms and across years—unfollowed me on social media. A few such incidents occurred.

Never abandon people who have lost power. There are deeper reasons for this—they cut to the heart of ethics, which are based in emotional solidarity.

Abandoning the degraded exposes you as something you would never wish to be seen as: a taker. It is also strategically foolish, not that I emphasize such points. People who lose power often regain it, as I have—sometimes in different, larger venues.

Be loyal. Loyalty is not corruption. It is reciprocity. It is a recognition of human oneness without inflicting injury on self or bending to unwanted relationship. It is saying: where the mob goes, I stand still. Mobs are not human. They are, in a sense, egregores: thought or energy forms of projected emotion.

I noted earlier that the castoff is considered under sacred protection in Hellenic religion. Remember this next time you shun someone. In ancient myth and parable, gods, demons, helpers, and genies often arrive as bedraggled strangers.

The moment "everyone" is against someone—watch carefully. Hive thinking is virtually never right. Or, rather, never wholly right. You can tell by the self-satisfied confidence with which it is held.

As a rule, accusations flatten complexity.

A twentieth-century spiritual teacher I admire, Vernon Howard (1918–1992), once told a roomful of students: "All I'm really trying to say is: why don't you just LEAVE PEOPLE ALONE! They've got problems of their own. They don't need your jokes or your smart remarks."

I used to revile seeing people canceled on Twitter. I felt as though every week was a grim dirge awaiting a new contestant subjected to the judgment of often-anonymous galley reapers. I found it sickening.

In that vein, Vernon had another expression. You will know its truth by the immediate urge to argue with it. It creates discomfort of the familiar without a price on anyone.

He often asked students not to react to such expressions, as you will to this one, but to write them down—and live with them for six months.

"Show me the victim and I'll show you the bully."

Is this a clarion to injustice? A dismissal of suffering? No, it is a reminder: to watch carefully. To suspend certainty. To question human nature.

"Zeus Hates Busybodies"

Excess blocks solutions. It substitutes ceaseless pursuit for natural cycles.

In his 1841 "Spiritual Laws," Ralph Waldo Emerson quotes a surviving fragment from a lost drama by Greek tragedian Euripides (c. 480–c. 406 B.C.): "Zeus hates busybodies and those who do too much."

I used to regard this, and still do, as an injunction against meddling, gossip, talebearing, and overtalking. But I neglected the second half: "those who do too much."

Emerson continues:

> The way of life is wonderful; it is by abandonment. The great moments of history are the facilities of performance through the strength of ideas, as the works of genius and religion are not the result of labor but of genius and inspiration.

In summer 2025, I spent a week at The Monroe Institute in Faber, Virginia. Founded by visionary broadcast executive and audio engineer Robert Monroe (1915–1995), it is both an ESP research facility and a personal growth center that employs sound to induce transcendental experience.

In a valuable and, in a certain sense, culminating exercise, we were invited to enter a deep state and ask five questions—things we needed to understand in descending importance. I am, for the first time in my writing, sharing the utmost response I received: "Do less."

That simple phrase contains a universe for me. It is, in a way, the "abandonment" Emerson invokes. I did not recall Emerson's passage until writing this chapter.

My life, perhaps like yours, is one of frenetic, almost harried activity. Readers often comment on my prolificness. I am proud of that—to a point. I over-grind. With that comes myriad problems versus solutions. For me, activity is automaticity. Overproduction is not a solution.

I have not read the channeled teachings of Abraham as communicated by Esther Hicks. From outside looking in, they never appealed to me. But an instructor I met at Monroe quoted something valuable.

As she recounted, an attendee on a Hicks cruise described the arduous nature of working as an "influencer," of continually pushing new content into the attention machine. Through Hicks, Abraham replied: "There is a Law of Attraction but not a Law of Assertion."

Those terms are not mine. But I see where perfervid activity, unleavened by passivity, fails to reconcile.

Solution, it must be recalled, means dissolving—the one gives way to an admixture, or reconciling whole. Constant activity ("those who do too much") is like adding but never congealing. Emerson's call for abandonment sings the song of Zeus, of Tao, of alchemy, of Zen—of life acting versus the individual constantly pushing.

Hold Your Ground

Having cautioned against ceaseless activity, I now introduce what some might see as a contradiction. It is not. It is a paradox. The quickest progress on the path is made by those who sustain paradox. "Every stick has two ends," Gurdjieff wrote.

Your greatest means of deliverance is persistence. Gurdjieff is quoted to this effect in chapter one. I have probed the metaphysical dimensions of persistence in *Practical Magick* and *The Sixth Sense* and I will not repeat that here. I now consider persistence from a more naturalistic perspective.

About thirty-five years ago, in my mid-twenties, I was treasurer of the youth section of the Democratic Socialists of America. A work friend on whom I had a crush—always one's toughest critic—said to me in reference to the fall of the Soviet Union, "What are you *doing* now?"

Her comment evinced tone deafness, a universal problem—in this case to my passionate distinction between democracy and authoritarianism. (Kids always dote on the big picture!) I write these words, however, to venture a different point. There is no politics in it. Zohran Mamdani's 2025 mayoral victory in New York—arguably the most significant electoral win for a socialist in U.S. history—occurred about twenty-four hours before this writing. That, unknowingly, is what I was "doing" then—building an organization in its darkest days in hopes of future utility.

Life is cyclical. Changes arrive long after efforts. The Wheel of Fortune as depicted in Tarot conveys a principle about the cyclical nature of experience. The wheel's rotations whisper to purposefully remain in place.

If you are earnestly and diligently working, training, drilling, rehearsing, preparing, and doing your labor, the Wheel of Fortune dictates that, eventually and inevitably, the cycle of rise and fall will reach you where you stand. In time, this natural force lifts your fortunes. It also lowers them. The lifting and lowering are, however, tempered by the quality of your work.

Eliphas Lévi's (1810–1875) 1850 rendering of the Wheel of Fortune

Let me also note something to those who are egregiously suffering. Never discount the possibility—entirely real—of extraordinary change, occurring suddenly. Life visits remarkable and unexpected events on us all the time. Such as a tormentor dying or vanishing from your experience. Does that sound morbid? Not to the threatened person. As much as we are victims of repetition and tragedy, we are also, in the course of time, recipients of absurdly good news. The miraculous is as much a part of life as the catastrophic. This is lawful. It is not fanciful to wait for welcome and dramatic turns of events; it is practical.

In essence, all things abide what might be called a Law of Cycles, which dictates that events within and without you change, flow, and renew like seasons, tides—or planetary revolutions, to which we now turn.

Mercury Retrograde

Astrology endures because its insights—whether causative or correlative (an ancient debate)—are reasonably accurate, a fact lost on those who feel strongly about movies they haven't seen. Its cycles can bring solutions.

"Astrology—the vital aspect of astronomy—is integrated in a synthesis that represents myth," wrote esoteric Egyptologist Isha Schwaller de Lubicz, wife of R.A. Schwaller, in *Her-Bak: Egyptian Initiate* (1956), "and should not be considered as a separate philosophical speculation as our rational mentality would lead us to believe."

While completing this chapter in fall 2025, earth entered a powerful cycle in Western astrology called Mercury Retrograde. About three occur yearly, during which Mercury appears to reverse its orbit due to a wobble in earth's axis. This is considered a time of reversals; but reversals can bring fixes.

I was born under Mercury Retrograde. I do not fear its mechanics. For one thing, those of us born under its influence age backwards. It infamously coincides with communication snafus, tech glitches, and disrupted travel. All true enough, in my experience. But there exists an esoteric aspect of Mercury Retrograde, which is richer and overlooked.

First, a bit of historical background. Astronomers in ancient Mesopotamia identified the optical phenomenon of Mercury Retrograde as early as the seventh century B.C. But interpretation of this celestial interval as disruptor of transportation and communication is more modern. An early such reference appears in William Lilly's 1647 *Christian Astrology*: "A Retrograde Planet . . . denotes ill in the Question, discord and much contradiction." References also appear in the mid-1700s in British agricultural almanacs read by farmers who believed planetary motions influence planting seasons.

Early twentieth-century astrologer Alan Leo (1860–1917) presaged how we view Mercury Retrograde today. Leo's wife Bessie wrote in a 1919 biography of her husband:

> It will be noticed that Mercury was retrograde at birth. This probably hampered the native in early life and prevented opportunities for intellectual development, but by progression Mercury became direct again at the age of 13, when, no doubt, many of the hindrances were removed.

Leo, like me, was a Mercury-Retrograde baby. According to the theory of progressions—where a day represents a year—my natal Mercury stationed direct at age nineteen, which coincides with my inceptive dedication to journalism.

Mercury Retrograde is not merely an interval of glitches. Rather, it must be considered a period of psychical unwinding: of self, relationships, and life patterns. Knots can be undone. People may reemerge from your past, directly or indirectly resurrecting unsettled business, whether emotional, relational, or practical. Resolutions may appear. Old ideas, undeveloped and abandoned, may return.

I consider Mercury Retrograde a healthful, if jarring, disruption of conceptualized linear time. It is a period of rough-hewn renewal, when problems retract and solutions newly surface. Mercury, the cosmic messenger, is a trickster. Mercury Retrograde is his high season. Do not impede his work.

As a rule: everything in nature is useful. Never discount her methods for presenting solutions. Especially when they bear no resemblance to expected, idealized, or prejudicial forms of deliverance. This is the wand of Mercury Retrograde.

* * *

If there is a Law of Solutions it is that expectation rarely holds them. The deceptively ordinary or offputtingly unfamiliar is how most fixes appear. When you discover solutions, as you will, they often prove simple, sweeping, and, sometimes, so natural that nothing seems to have happened at all.

When I was young, the Rebbe Menachem Mendel Schneerson (1902–1994) looked me in the eye. It is not an experience you forget. I want to share one small statement he made. The rebbe spoke these words to Talmudic scholar Adin Steinsaltz (1937–2020) who showed up at one of his talks unannounced. It appears atop this chapter: "Good things always arrive unexpectedly."

THREE

Do You Seek Truth—Or Happiness?

Possibilities enter your life through clarity. Hence, this book is, in part, an exercise in self-definition.

Never confuse truth with happiness.

The two may conflate. But not always.

We frequently hear that people crave truth—and, connectedly, community. I challenge that.

"People are just hungry for truth." A woman loosely connected to the Gurdjieff work once emphatically pronounced this to me at a lunch with Jacob Needleman, a senior figure in that work.

Afterwards I told him, "I would like to meet these people. Because I certainly cannot find them when I need to organize a cleaning or grocery-shopping team."

I was referencing activities within the work that are common necessities of maintenance for meetings, spaces, and activities. You cannot function as a group without these things. Yet phone call after phone call generally met with "maybes"—a coward's "no." (I used to call it a "slow-motion no." That is generous.)

I apply this same critique to myself. Do I want truth? I am not so sure. For one thing, I am no longer in that work, which I consider a rare and authentic current of truth. I had my reasons for leaving. Some were good. Some were probably selfish. I am unsure.

I once said in a group meeting, "What we call 'happiness' is often resistance to the work." By this I meant the intentional labors and suffering that Gurdjieff prescribed as necessary payment in life. I abide that. But my statement was then and is today too narrow.

It can be argued that redolence is not happiness. Seen from a certain perspective, it is bondage. One must beware of coveting the nicest cell in the prison.

Still, the happiness-seeking person is warranted in his or her wishes. Pursuing happiness is not a miscarried search for truth. It is an indirect means of approaching truth. Further, one's lived definition of happiness may have sound and good reasons behind it. I cannot evaluate what proves intimately necessary in the life of another.

I know woman in New York City who was raised in poverty by a mentally ill mother out West. She is the most splendid purveyor of fashion and appearance—

sans money!—I know. She exemplifies authentic and ingenious chicness. "I realized," she once said, "that if I look rich, people will treat me like I'm rich." Only those ignorant of want could misunderstand her happy insight; high thinkers and divines would remand her to customary wisdom.

I must mention as an aside something that occurred after I wrote those words. A small group of friends gathered in late 2025 to celebrate her birthday at a Manhattan restaurant. She reserved a booth that was personally meaningful to her. After promising it, however, the restaurant gave it away to a movie star. I witnessed my friend innocently induce Scarlett Johansson—a model of graciousness—to volunteer the booth while a very important waiter named Vinnie (or is it Vinny?) stood by fuming.

* * *

We hear a lot about knowing what you want. It seems obvious. It is not.

The rite of *self-disclosure* is powerful because it cuts to the heart of the chief human vehicle: desire.

We spend our lives struggling against desire. This is not necessarily without reason. Some desires can kill us. Some can harm others. But most are self-contained—albeit not without risk. Absence of risk or embarrassment ensures familiarity and repetition.

I want to share a statement that I do not understand. I understand it in words and concepts. But not in my bones. Nor do you. This chapter is an attempt for us both, writer and reader, to peer a bit more fully into the keyhole that this statement supplies. It is aspirational in conventional terms but it can be applied generally, as can all truths.

Lord John Pentland (1907–1984) was philosopher G.I. Gurdjieff's selected student to build his work in the U.S. Lord Pentland, who, as founder of the American British Electric Corporation, was on familiar terms with earned wealth, stated:

> The hardest thing to convince people of is a fact only the very rich know: the way to make money is to do exactly what you want to do and to do it exactly the way you want to do it.*

Simple in framing, complex in application—another hallmark of truth.

I believe that within his statement lies the principle of *passivity*. It is the opposite of how we usually think, which is in terms of activity. Gurdjieff and many philosophers, ancient and modern, including Nietzsche, stated that three forces devise creation: active, passive, and reconciling.

* "Religion and Money," *Gurdjieff International Review*, Fall 2005

I am ceaselessly active. I have told you my motto: *Try* or as put on a recent sticker, *Die Trying*. But am I right? It may depend on one's stage of life. If I neglected activity, I would not have become a writer. But today the active effort can prove a barrier to my wishes. Through continual effort, I sometimes push into professional tasks and settings I neither want nor like. Effort creates ersatz desire. Fear is active, for me at least.

Pushing, too, is active. But life may call for passivity. Constantly loading the circuits may prove a barrier to the very thing you want. This recalls the earlier statement I received at The Monroe Institute, "Do less."

We do not like the term passivity. But our dislike is conditioned. Without passivity there would exist no womb, no subconscious, no soil, no fertility, no meditation, no silence, no lotus, and so on. Passivity is not secondary. It is the current of life. It is the descending stream of wisdom, without which our traditions would not exist in taught form.

* * *

When I was a young editor, maybe age twenty-five, I had lunch with a friendly literary agent named Bob Silverstein. I hated most agents. I found them snobbish and dishonest. I could relax with Bob. He was a late-middle-aged man with a quick smile, no airs, and an athletic, trim build that bespoke someone who enjoyed physicality.

For whatever reason, I asked him why he became an agent. He explained that as a younger man he did not know what to do with his life. He had no idea how he would earn a living. He asked himself the question implicit in this chapter: *what do I like?*

With disarming sincerity, he said: "I like sex." How could that be a career? Bob was a letters guy. He had an idea. At that time, certain porn films, including *Deep Throat* and *The Devil in Miss Jones*, were experiencing nationwide theatrical distribution and popularity. This is the kind of American decline written about in a John Cheever short story. It is also the *zeitgeist*—irresistible. Bob decided to write novelizations of these popular porn movies. Although that publishing niche is less prominent today than it once was, novelizations of popular movies, such as *Fatal Attraction* and even *Hoffa*, routinely hit bestseller lists. It was big business. Bob's novelizations of porn became hits. He earned enough money to buy a nice house in the Hudson Valley, where he could play tennis nearly every day. His literary agenting grew from his literary-porn business.

Principles of both passivity and activity appear in Bob's story. The idea requires passivity, or receiving. The execution—too often neglected—requires activity, or at least activity within the passive current.

A billionaire investor once told me and a huddle of listeners: "There are a lot of great ideas out there. I look for great execution more than great ideas. Great execution is much rarer than great ideas."

I took that statement so fully to heart that I grew dedicated to activity. And, again, it may have been seasonally necessary. But try to imagine the passivity within activity. As I write these words, I realize that quality appears in these chapters. They are written from experience and great effort, now in repose. Their writing flowed quickly. I am proud of these chapters. They tell the truth. They travel with, not against, the current.

* * *

We do not tell ourselves what we desire, or allow ourselves to feel it, because it may be embarrassing, especially within. We internalize peer pressure and conditioned ideas to the point where they seem organic rather than customary.

I am not issuing a statement of ultimacy. Life is dynamic and requires different approaches at different times. The best way to kill wisdom is by rendering it into a procedure. Hence, I do not want you to over-parse Lord Pentland's statement. I want us all to sit with it.

From there, ask yourself at a private moment: *What do I want in life?* Be exquisitely unembarrassed. Be private. (Spilling our guts to others dilutes our wishes and invites idiot commentary.) When the answer arrives—truth facilitates speed—you will immediately consider it unrealistic. That is conditioned. Bob did not plan to become a porn star, movie producer, photographer, or sex worker. Those were not his proclivities. Again, he was a letters guy. It worked.

I do not know that it will always work. But think of this: the exercise I propose is, in itself, an act of passivity. You are not pushing. You are receiving. Permit it.

I am not writing this chapter to tell you that one or another aim is better. That would be a joke played, above all, on myself. I cannot possibly know what is meaningful, or why, in your life. Those who believe that they can prescribe what constitutes the good life are often blindly repeating translation upon translation of hand-me-down religious and ethical wisdom that they cannot read in the original language in which such dictums were written (if the originals still exist).

My point, rather, is to ask you to know what you want. Really know. With vivifying certainty. Personal verity, when it arrives, is often embarrassing. This is because verity defies internalized peer pressure. It comes as the kind of self-acknowledgment that you are leery of repeating to another. You are right to be leery.

Odds are that another person, whether spouse, shrink, friend, or hallowed guide, will destroy it—because it does not match whatever is inside him. Agreement or disagreement is the lowest form of engagement with an idea. It is also the most overwhelmingly common.

If you want truth—and happiness—start exactly from yourself and with your most private wishes. Do not be concerned, at least for now, whether you can act on those wishes. Acting is another matter. But at least know them. Private yearnings—sexual, financial, relational, artistic, physical—lie behind so much of what happens to you.

I often note the importance of a critical life aim. This sometimes prompts an objection: why not opt for a more Taoist "just be" attitude? I contend that our aims, desires, and wishes rest in the emotions. They assert themselves with or without our awareness. Marrying that pull to intent or intellect provides at least some modicum of awareness and direction—because that aim will, with or without us, take its due. Other times people say that they have difficulty locating or, in light of what I have just written, acknowledging their aim. That difficulty may be due to peer-driven embarrassment. In fairness, the difficulty of defining an aim is innate to human nature. We are in disparate parts. What do we serve? How do we know? I have no universal answers, but I often say that one well-selected aim, such as procuring money, can cover many bases, including caring for people around you.

My personal aim has recently shifted. I am not being cagey but I will not share it—yet—because my arrival at this new aim is so recent and delicate. I am not ready to submit my self-insight to scrutiny. I reached my new aim because I encountered the feeling that a previously cherished and long-abided aim proved too reliant on other people. This book leaves you little doubt of what I think about "other people," the crowd, "they"—the dominant human force—save a precious, sensitive fraction. Hence, I need an aim that is not only more self-directed but more *foundational* to what my prior one enunciated.

When you realize the thing you really want, you will know its authenticity by the occurrence of what might be called meaningful coincidences. "A coincidence is lawful," a senior colleague once told me. I am uncertain that is always true—but I am sufficiently haunted by her statement to take it seriously. Watch for this in your life.

I will say further: happiness, if not truth (or not always), is relational. The times in life when you are happy almost certainly coincide with, and emerge from, the company you keep. Whatever your path, never submit to company that makes you feel inferior. This may place you before a great challenge. Do not shrink from this challenge.

A reader once wrote me, in a splendid candor, that her mother had emotionally tormented her for her entire life. After her mother died, she said, she felt truly happy—and never once looked back. Can you see how ersatz-seekers would rush to steal her truth? To redirect it? To offer her, unasked, a countering line of thought from *Bartlett's Divine Quotations*?

I applaud her honesty. Honesty is happiness, too.

I sometimes prescribe a thought-exercise. I use it myself. As should be clear, everything that I write, I use. My search and my work are one. Imagine that a genie offers you one wish. But it is conditioned. In voicing your wish, you must tell the genie the *absolute truth*—or you will lose everything.

What is it?

Use it right now or at your earliest private and uninterrupted moment. If you respond with psychical truth—unifying intellect, emotion, and physicality—you will receive a gift. When it arrives, accept it.

I close on another statement of Lord Pentland's: "Rich people think passively, yes?"

FOUR

"The Body Has to See It Can Be Told What to Do"

Our private resolutions fail because we exist in pieces. You will find that theme throughout this book.

Mind, emotions, and body travel separate and discordant tracks.

Were this not so, there would be no addictions, stupid violence (emotional and physical), war—and broken vows, above all to self.

The only thing over which we have any control is our attention, a facet of intellect. This control is limited and partial. Emotions constantly steal our attention, as do physicality and sexuality.

But attention exists. When it functions, we experience, fleetingly, the closest proximity to normal being as described in currents of esoteric philosophy.

* * *

You, like me, perhaps at a younger time, knew the experience of blowing an exam, meeting, or job interview by oversleeping. For a pissant few minutes of sleep, or another bite of unnecessary food, the body steals our birthright, as Esau's was for a bowl of stew—the story's esoteric meaning.

As we mature, we generally awaken on time—but struggle with other factors: over-eating, debt spending, too much booze or weed (me), gambling, and so on.

In nearly every case, the body is in control. You must try—*try*—to take it back.

"The body has to see it can be told what to do," Jacob Needleman told me. He was drawing on principles of G.I. Gurdjieff.

Within this simple statement—*the body has to see it can be told what to do*—lies your destiny, if you have any.

* * *

Addictions—life-threatening compulsions—are beyond the scope of this chapter, or so I believe. I address myself to matters of common consumption.

In such cases, I do not counsel abstinence or self-denial. Nor do I discourage pharmacological help. I simply and decisively ask that you *use your mind more.* Tell your body what to do.

I say body, not emotions. Emotions are faster and stronger than intellect (and, beyond instinctive impulses, body too). When disturbed, emotions are a kicking horse over which intellect (the driver) has no reins and body is in service. The body has its own dominance and claims, but it is the carriage in Gurdjieff's horse-driver-carriage metaphor.

I posit small steps working with attention and body. Find yourself—as a self—however briefly, in that.

Man is a machine, an automaticity imagining its independence. Independence does not exist—without development.

Attention is your fitful revolt against this mechanized sleep. It is your one tool.

* * *

This story may be apocryphal, but it has vintage within the Gurdjieff work. When the teacher first visited the U.S. in 1924, a reporter asked: "Mr. Gurdjieff, what is your message for the people of America in one sentence?"

He replied: "Think."

There is a danger in this story. Everyone who reads it believes it is intended for someone else. Everyone who reads it believes it is political or social in implication.

Thinking means *observing self.* Everything starts with that function.

This suggests the depth of the familiar Delphic maxim, *know thyself.* It further indicates the interior of the Hermetic dictum, *as above, so below.* And the esotericism of the Scriptural, *God created man in his own image.*

Familiarity obfuscates the interior and scale of these statements.

* * *

Can you sit still for ten minutes? Try. If not, you cannot think. I have no illusions that more than one or two people reading this will try. I know this from self. And do not dare quote Yoda to me. If man could *do*, we wouldn't be in this mess to begin with.

For fifteen minutes—no, make it just ten—switch your dominant hand. You cannot. You will not even try. Should you, you will see that.

That is the limit of our thinking.

What I describe is apparently small in scale and lacking visible consequence—consider how this situation plays out across your existence. This is among the reasons Gurdjieff deemed man *asleep*—not metaphorically but actually.

One night years ago, I was interviewed by a host who was late—this was considered cool—and unprepared. He glanced over the jacket copy of my *Occult America* before commencing a "dialogue" in front of a live audience of cross-legged onlookers, eager to hear something of substance. I referenced humanity's sleep. He asked the group, "How many of you believe that's true?" A small minority of hands went up. Do you know when you are asleep? It is almost (not quite) laughable.

* * *

Wisdom, like other good things, arrives unexpectedly. A cosmetician recently told me: "Beauty is pain."

I was struck by the truth of her statement. For example, eschewing food is pain. So is weightlifting or running. Even cosmetic procedures (to which she directly referred) are pain.

I hate not feeling full. When hunger strikes, my mind is weakest. Here is exactly where the body *must be told what to do*—and not just that: the body, itself a brain in Gurdjieff's schema, must *see that it can be told*. This is attention.

We are limited by physicality yet mistreat our bodies. In the West, we desire the feeling of fullness more than the vitality of incomplete satiety. I drink alcohol and smoke weed nearly every night, so I am hardly ascetic on the point. A student complained to Gurdjieff of ennui or general unhappiness. He told him to leave just a bit of food uneaten at every meal.

Here is a very delicate needle to thread. I am not sure if I should thread it. But the path must include experiment. Follow the theme I develop. Gurdjieff called it "riding the Devil's back." I do not use the term *devil*—an exoteric misnomer—and I do not ride a deity's back. I seek an ally. But I bow to this framing and proceed from it.

I once helped my teacher clean out his father-in-law's library. I hungrily eyed a box marked, "Occult Books." He knew. "If you help me the rest of the afternoon," he said, "you can have that box." I gamely agreed.

I got home, eager to open my box. It had been mislabeled. These were not occult books at all but rather books from the traditions, ranging from Tibetan Buddhism to Orthodox Christianity. "Can you imagine my disappointment?" I later joked to his wife, "What have I to do with the traditions!"

Read no intention into this story. I recognize the after-the-fact temptation to do so, which is always present. We explain accident that way. In any case, I kept a few of the books and gave away others. But the prospective reward had moved me.

A meditation teacher once told me that she thought it was okay to pay kids to meditate. "Why not?" she said. "We give kids allowances for other things, like doing their homework or finishing chores." She understood human nature with an admirable absence of sentimentality.

You have unmet needs in life. *Use them as a goad.* Do not place yourself above such practice. Trick yourself if you must. A trick is a carriage, like the body. Ride it.

What I describe is, in a sense, transmutation—*lead into gold* of alchemical tradition, albeit on a fragmentary scale.

* * *

Here, as elsewhere, I am dragging esoteric wisdom into the low tide of application. I do so intentionally. That is the point of *Esoterika*. It is a downward motion. We have no choice. The hour is late and nothing about humanity is getting better.

There exists no hope for humanity, as a whole. There exists precious little possibility for an individual, almost to the point of nothing. Argue with it all you want. It is true. You feel that.

From the perspective of esoteric wisdom, humanity occupies a declining octave. In Vedic terms, this might be seen as the cycle of Kali Yuga, considered an era of conflict and spiritual degradation beginning in 3,102 B.C. and concluding in 428,899 A.D., lasting 432,000 conventional years, a number with surprising congruences in other religious systems. It is, for example, implied in Norse myth by the description of Valhalla's 540 doors with 800 warriors, or *einherjar*—

poetically, "those who fight alone"—issuing from each door for the final battle (540×800), a convergence discussed by Joscelyn Godwin in *Atlantis and the Cycles of Time.*

What I note gives an idea of the vastness of cosmic cycles considered by Madame H.P. Blavatsky (1831–1891) in her 1888 *The Secret Doctrine* and Gurdjieff in his magisterial 1950 *Beelzebub's Tales to His Grandson,* books more read about than read. Gurdjieff asked that his cathedral-sized opus be read three times. I, like your middle-school English teacher, always know who hasn't "read the book." I detected this years ago in a bestseller on the "secret history of the world." My publishing boss studied my face: why did I not like this successful book? Why did I not want us to reprint it? He thought me jealous, a projection. Not that—but this: such books as Gurdjieff's and Blavatsky's should not be referenced sans reading. This degrades ethics and worsens sleep.

Cynics, who have no other reference, consider idealism weakness. Submitting to this judgment, in esoteric Sufism and elsewhere, is sometimes called *the path of blame.* It is for "those who fight alone."

Given what I have written, *why try*? We must. We cannot desist or life grows unbearable. We cannot stand the debt of not trying, of not paying for our existence.

You are a living being. Automaticity will not pay for your existence. Those who shirk this debt, like all debts, are wholly lost and vacant.

Now: think. In so doing, show your body that it can be told what to do. Try.

FIVE

Identification Is Not the Problem

I opened with the challenge of a wish. My teacher once said that if he could receive a single wish, he would ask for a day without identification. "Just to know how it feels," he added.

Identification, a concept most sharply developed in the work of G.I. Gurdjieff and also heard in Buddhism and other traditions, means associating self with thing, such as career or money.

I note two things in my teacher's statement:

1. I believe he meant it. He was more committed to the search than I am.
2. He dedicated his life to the search. If identification seemed so entrenched to him, consider what any seeker faces.

But I wonder: if identification—*self as thing*—is implacable, or practically so, can it be considered a problem? Or is identification innate to the human situation, like the need for shelter?

Rather than eluding identification, there may exist a different approach; one that acknowledges the suffering of fixation—while transmuting it.

In the light of spiritual tradition, identification is abrogation of self. It is an artifice of human crisis. As such, identification can, within plausible bounds, be *given up for something better*. This is the seeker's aim.

I do not know, nor does anyone reading these words know, what non-identification feels like. The closest we achieve is the state that occurs upon experiencing emotional shock, such as the death of a loved one. At that instant, rote multiplicities of thought, emotion, and physicality are interrupted. In such cases, a *no* means *no* and a *yes* means *yes*.

That state fades and cannot be clung to.

But I have recently wondered about the prospect, in ordinary hours, of dedicating oneself to necessary tasks with which one does not identify. In such cases, would intellect prevail? Would action prove unclouded by grabbiness or frivolity?

* * *

When I worked in publishing, I knew a successful literary agent named Richard Pine. His father, Arthur Pine, was an old-school talent manager and universally loved man. Richard was tough—but ethical and approachable. I always liked (and slightly feared) him.

One day at lunch, I noted that he had two or maybe three books simultaneously on *The New York Times Bestseller List*.

"Richard," I asked, "tell me your secret. How do you do it?"

He replied: "Try not to love anything too much. I always figure, if something slips away, something better will come. It's kind of Zen."

I respect Richard's statement. But: Is what he describes generally and practically cultivable?

It seems to me that for most people, not according to some posited ideal but as they really exist, the absence of identification—in the ordinary sense (I return to the broader spiritual one) produces boredom and indifference, resulting in mediocrity and slog.

* * *

I dedicated twenty-seven years to corporate publishing. During that time, I witnessed executives, financiers, media reporters, and informed authors wonder why publishing's finances seemed perpetually precarious. Some of it had to do with limited audiences. But there was another factor.

In my experience, no matter what efforts prevailed, profit margins at a sound trade publisher always hovered at nine percent. That is not a bad outcome. Yet it proved resistant to growth and hence at odds with shareholder demand.

Moreover, the book business saw lots of fallow periods and dips. The worst in my era was dissolution of the chain retailer Border's following the 2008 Great Recession. It hurt books and the nation alike.

I was not in the room, so I must flag the following statement as second hand. It was repeated to me by a sales manager for Penguin, who was in the room. Prior to its collapse, Borders convened a meeting to reassure creditors, including publishers, that bills would be paid. My friend knew the end was imminent, however, when the CEO then dismissed eBooks as a fad.

I got fired in 2017, the second (and last) of two times book conglomerates expelled me. So, I knew periods of plenty and lack, though I reckon my ledger is in black ink. I was an acquisitions editor and, eventually, a division vice-president and editor-in-chief. I had perspective.

I noticed something that I whispered to colleagues. The aforementioned financiers, journalists, and executives had this in common: they were not on the shop floor. On the shop floor, I witnessed roughly five percent of staff row to keep the boat steady. Everyone else was doing something, anything, other than issue and sell good books.

I will tell an old story that still strikes me with near-disbelief. In 2001, our offices were near the financial district and the events of 9/11 were viscerally felt and, by some, witnessed from office windows. In the months ahead, a top executive was tasked with drawing up emergency plans to keep the company running in the event of another crisis. One later came in COVID. Reviewing the plans, I noticed that they covered all kinds of communication mechanisms, author-agent-media contact lists, and workflow charts. One thing was missing. How to get our product—the book—from printer to market. To my knowledge, no one flagged it. That was publishing.

Then and now, it struck me that the unnamed factor in publishing's shaky fortunes is, as a staffing matter, *paucity of talent*. My maxim: when diagnosing problems, start with the shop floor.

I am unsure but I relate that issue, indirectly, to identification or its lack, i.e., to people with no emotion, intellect, or skin in the game. They have little to prove or lose.

The words you are now reading, like the books I published, would not exist without identification—by which I mean: seeing self within task.

There exist higher forms of dedication than identification. But I am addressing the middling nature of the human situation.

* * *

I recently met an artist I venerate. I told him, "Ninety percent of what I write is produced to prove I am not stupid."

It is a naked admission. I make it because—what is the search without transparency?

What I write reflects identification. At age sixty, I doubt I will ever move past it. Pain and expression are intimately linked. On those terms, I ask myself whether identification is really a problem—can there exist a problem without a solution?—or if its fixational qualities beckon something greater.

As noted, my teacher, now dead, wished for a day—just one day—to elude identification.

His wish is not mine.

My wish is victory: in career, artistry, and expression.

I may have disappointed him.

But sincerity, it seems to me, is perhaps the one facet of life that exists beyond identification. It is the bridge of incident to creativity and questioning.

I cannot know a life without identification. But nor can I sustain a life without sincerity—and the quality of attention it brings.

My life is locked into identification as fixation, which produces pain. But attention to that pain—and its relationship to creativity, impeccability, and effort—may represent the sole exit we are granted.

Identification is permanent, as a practical matter. But it can, through attention and sincerity, be transmuted into impeccability.

In a dictum I used earlier, Jacob Needleman warned: "Do not long for the nicest cell in the prison."

I do not question his principle, but its application. We are animated by laws and forces over which we have no control. That is unchanging.

For my part, I am not picking a lock, digging a tunnel, or scaling a wall. I cannot. My effort is transforming circumstance, or "the prison" in his term, from within.

Within impeccability lies subversion. Impeccability is an alchemical adjunct to identification. The desultory will never possess nor understand it. They call it perfectionism or other epithets. Even on such terms, I want perfectionism in surgeons, pilots, engineers—and publishers. But that is not what I mean.

A singular energy arises from impeccability. You will feel its self-unifying forces. They are known through experience alone.

For this to occur, however, you must function in environments that either summon or lead to dedication and impeccability. Physical safety is a factor—not something possessed by all. You may not currently be there. Depending on geography, however, this is a solvable crisis. It presents, at least, an authentic and worthy effort, which itself summons the energies I describe.

* * *

My teacher told me a story that came back to me only after completing this chapter—though I must have recalled it sensorily or emotionally while writing it.

At some point, he was attending a period of work with people dedicated to Gurdjieff's ideas.

The house they stayed in had a staircase in need of repair. He worked on it into the night.

Hours into the task, another man came to him with a blanket and pillow. "Here," he said, "you're so identified with those stairs you should sleep with them."

My teacher told me, "He was wrong. Because a man has to be involved with something."

Postscript: On Stupidity

Earlier I mentioned fear of stupidity. That bears final unpacking.

I once made a painful confession to my teacher. I am not sure it is correct, but it was stated sincerely.

Beyond rank and position, I told him, the tough truth is that success in life stems from raw, quantifiable intellect, the kind tested for in standardized exams. His silence signaled agreement.

A friend of mine in the physics doctoral program at Columbia disagreed. He tutored people for tests so he was in a position to know. But he also had what I do not: intellect that aces abstract analysis and logic problems.

In *The Prince*, Machiavelli writes that there exist three kinds of intellect: 1) Those who can do the thing itself, which is excellent. 2) Those who can judge the thing, which is good. 3) Those who can neither do nor judge, which is worthless.

The third kind signals not only absence of skill but, crucially, inability of judgment.

I confessed that day that I possess the second kind. That was, however, before I rediscovered myself as a writer. I now claim the first—but without disavowing my confession or personal disclosure.

From where, then, does the third kind, i.e., stupidity, emerge?

Ethics arise from the emotions. It seems to me that stupidity does, too.

Stupidity is the intellectual equivalent of a program missing a dot or dash—hence, everything comes out wrong, every insight is off-kilter. This is not attributable to a paucity of quantifiable intellect. I attest that much. Then what causes stupidity, sometimes in evidently educated and even accomplished people? It is coarseness of emotion. This interrupts integration, context, and doubt.

This suggests why some people can never be convinced of anything, nor can their support for bad ideas or their disdain for good ones be leavened or slackened. They lack emotional receptivity to suspended judgment. Departures, when they occur, prove temporary. Departures imply motion.

A professor of mine, film historian James Harvey, once said, "You know, Mitchell"—he and my mother called me that—"the older I get, the more I realize there are really two kinds of people: those who like where they come from and those who do not." He meant this in terms of lineage; but it says, I think, the same thing I do here.

How do you deal with stupidity? The same way I counsel dealing with cruelty: escape it. Immediately and without qualification. In a world of limited time and endless communication, do not damn a stone. Step around it. If you cannot, vow internally that you will at the first opportunity.

A stone will always remain a stone. It is its nature.

SIX

What Is Yours to Give

Our spiritual culture, particularly in its popular iterations, often focuses on the theme of *service*. This concept obfuscates intent and effectiveness. It translates too readily into toothless memes and self-claims.

I state the following from a spiritual—by which I mean extraphysical—perspective. There is, I trust, zero cynicism in it. If anything, I consider what I propose tough idealism.

Money and time are the only things you have to give another person.

That principle is not mine. It was said by a senior figure in the Gurdjieff work and repeated to me by Jacob Needleman. Upon hearing it, I knew it was true. I knew because I, like you, immediately want to argue with it. I want to argue because the principle shatters sentimentality regarding itself as depth.

Once upon a time, a prominent New Age organization expelled me from its speaking, media, and prison-ministry work. This came in the wake of a whispering campaign that I am a Satanist. That misunderstood—and correct—shorthand, unpacked in later chapters, conceals a deeper truth. Before I was shitcanned, an elder member told me, "We are about service."

I am not about service. I consider service a dodge. When someone I care about is in need, I give them money. Or, if required, time. The latter is more difficult for me.

Money does not relieve underlying factors. It cannot heal a sick person. But it does bring solutions. Time also brings solutions. Good vibes, thoughts, prayers, affirmations, distance healing, psychical whatever, are often done for the subject—not the object of need. More often than not, they are pageantry.

An older friend and teacher was recovering from knee surgery. I routinely visited him. "What can I bring?" I asked. He might name foods that were unhealthy but that I knew comforted him. One day, I elected to bring him a low-calorie version of the chocolate milk he requested. I was, I thought, thinking of his health. "You were thinking of yourself," he said. He was right.

I watched him painfully wean himself off post-surgery opioids. Who I am to determine which chocolate milk he drinks? When giving, give without condition or supposed lesson. Socialist and philosopher Michael Harrington (1928–1989) disdained the Salvation Army. "I don't think someone should have to say a prayer to get a bowl of soup," he said.

When I was younger, I occasionally attended a New Thought church. Like most churches, they passed a collection basket. A woman in a floor-length fur coat—this cannot be made up—would hold the basket and wave her hand over it in blessing, but drop in no cash. "What I have to give is more than money," she told a friend. Well, give both. One can be counted on.

* * *

It disgusts me when people hoard money, especially in small sums. I recognize costs and I recognize emotions. But giving away money is possibly the only measure of making positive and actual impact in another's life. If one believes, as I do, in reciprocity (not always detectable) then the benefit clearly redounds.

If you want to know who you are, consider how you tip. It says everything. I recognize that the tipping economy is problematic. But until that is fixed, tipping is the chief source of income for many service workers. I have witnessed, as have most people reading this, wealthy individuals parse tips on restaurant meals. Would you cast away your humanity for an extra $1.80? Most of us would.

My mother and her mother used to pinch tips and harass waitstaff. My grandmother, a mean, gravelly voiced woman, would undertip with the epithet, "That's plenty." These were not poor people. "If you can afford to eat in a restaurant," I told the former, "you can afford to tip well." Those words can go on my gravestone.

As a young boy, I once watched my mother boss around a shoe salesman—and then buy nothing. She walked out while he was on his knees fitting another customer. I could see his eyes were watery. I apologize by treating service personnel as I wish to be treated.

I am better with money than with time. Hence, as a parent of two sons I attempt generosity to compensate for my periods of distraction writing or engaged in other selfish activities. It is flawed, but it is an effort.

For those who do not have money to give, time may be a help. For those with neither time nor money—an understandable predicament—a pass is given. Your life is so busy that you are already giving both. But do not dare claim that category without cause. That renders a life useless.

In Ford Madox Ford's (1873–1939) series of novels and adapted television drama *Parade's End*, the hero Christopher Tietjens is asked for a loan by a friend from a lower social rung. Christopher replies that he does not loan money—he gives his friend the money. The friend later betrays him. That is why the novel is about not the friend but Christopher. We fitfully recognize honor and nobility, even when we violate or pretend to it.

I once needed a bridge loan for a real-estate transaction. The amount was about $1,600. Well-off relatives loaned it to me. They charged me 6% interest and required me to sign a promissory note. I complied and returned it early with interest. I assume their stringency was due to fear that I would come back seeking more; they wanted to make a no-you-don't gesture. Money is a fount of fear.

Clinging to something—like money or food—for fear there will be "no more" is a crouching posture that can deform a life. Carlos Castaneda's *Journey to Ixtlan* (1972) presents this dialogue with his teacher don Juan:

> "To be unavailable means that you deliberately avoid exhausting yourself and others," he continued. "It means that you are not hungry and desperate, like the poor bastard that feels he will never eat again and devours all the food he can, all five quail!"
>
> Don Juan was definitely hitting me below the belt. I laughed and that seemed to please him. He touched my back lightly.
>
> "A hunter knows he will lure game into his traps over and over again, so he doesn't worry. To

> worry is to become accessible, unwittingly accessible. And once you worry you cling to anything out of desperation; and once you cling you are bound to get exhausted or to exhaust whoever or whatever you are clinging to."

This does not summon asceticism. Sometimes its opposite. In *Beelzebub's Tales to His Grandson*, Gurdjieff writes about a Russian merchant on a trip to market who buys books for his son. The purchase, already expensive, is heightened by the cost of wrapping and postage. No matter. The merchant says: "If you go on a spree then go the whole hog including the postage."

"Go the whole hog including the postage." That is a good guide for how to treat others in matters of money. I used to have an expression, "Don't pinch pennies on the backs of friends." Spend lavishly on another. Who knows? This hour could be your last. Remember what I wrote earlier about honoring strangers.

Several years before this writing, a duo of Vedic scholars sought my consultation on a work they were considering writing. Both are students of Maharishi Mahesh Yogi (1928–2008). I can say lots of significant things about this couple and their history. But I will limit myself to one episode.

I discussed the project with them in whatever fullness I could bring to the exchange. We parted. A friend reached out to say that they wished to remunerate me for my time and wanted to know a number. I mentioned the hourly rate I generally charge for professional consults and let it go. It did occur to me that the amount was perhaps prohibitive. After a great passage of time, I received a lovely note in the mail, with an elephant on the front—and the sum enclosed. There is something of the primal ethic in this.

As I have been alluding, the question of money on the path is perhaps the most fraught faced by seekers. I believe it is treated with greater complexity than is warranted. Money, sex, reliability, security—all themes of life are one theme: Do you keep your word?

Whether one uses techniques, from prosperity-gospel teachings to New-Age manifesting (I call it *selecting*), to procure money, and whether such things work—and it seems to me they do, albeit fitfully—is not the concern of this exploration. My concern is the ethic of money and spirituality.

The spiritual or religious seeker pursues a relationship, on whatever terms, with the nonlocal dimension of life, whether one conceives it as deific, quantum, contemplative, or all of these. The terms are secondary insofar as all of our means of relating to the unseen are metaphorical. We place names on events, like lightning or gravity. We witness these events in fragmentary form.

Money is like spirituality. Here, too, we ascribe it different names—e.g., gold, dollar, bitcoin—all to denote something that may not exist beyond perception. That said, money is nearly as vital as the air you are breathing. The world stands on money, security, and sexuality, often the latter two informed by the first.

In that light, to say, "I don't care about money" is virtually impossible.

Indeed, most of the time, most of us are intensely concerned with how to get more money. We stream into therapy, religion, self-help, etc., seeking truth whereas we often—not always—seek security. And sometimes more than security. We seek power, which money also is in the world. Education, health, beauty, art, travel, housing—all of these things, to greater or lesser degree, rely on money. To say money is not power is to understand little about power.

In the sense I describe it, money is, in fact, the medium of human exchange. How you handle it is who you are.

* * *

I like giving away money. I am not always able to do that. Do I do it because I am "generous"? Or because it is a means of control or influence? One night when I peer into the abyss, I will consider that question more fully. But the recipients certainly do not care—money fills their need. In that regard, the act is good—it is generative, productive, and useful.

My mother, who was intermittently cunning and foolish with money, made what I consider one of the most corrupt statements I have heard: "They're very generous—they can afford to be generous." She was speaking of a third-party in the family. There is no such thing as conditional generosity. Such a framing misconstrues the nature of generosity, which is personal connectedness and reciprocity. Without these traits, humanity would falter. Even a hardened materialist would agree, perhaps using the term security.

"The yoga of money," Jacob Needleman told me, "can mean giving or not giving." His point is that giving or withholding must be subject to intellect and not emotion alone. Jerry wrote a book called *Money and the Meaning of Life*. In it, he further noted that someone unaware of exactly how much money he has—right now—is probably unaware of most things in his life.

Ironically, Jerry was bad with money. A late-life divorce threw him into turmoil over money. He did not always deal with it in a dignified fashion. Stability abets money. If you wish to experience security around money, mind what I wrote earlier about reciprocity. There are exceptions to that but usually in the life of the very rich, which most of us are not.

* * *

Both rich and struggling people have stolen money from me. I tend to take people at their word—we all project our ethics onto others, something to watch out for. One of the most dangerous things you can do in life is project your capacity to hold a question onto another. This feeds false trust. Even more dangerous, another person can read this quality in you, without quite knowing what it is, and posture as holding a question, when he holds none. *People imitate idealists and seekers.*

I have grown close to people who betrayed me. They reflected back what they fuzzily detected in me—and I bought it. Temporarily. After the ache of betrayal, I slowly, haltingly realized the artifice I had accepted. Projection blinds us.

I find it semi-funny (only semi) when people accuse me of that groan-worthy term *grifter* for my advocacy of parapsychology research. As a rule—not to my liking—I earn next-to-nothing for my work on parapsychology. The accuser reveals himself, less as a grifter (he, too, earns nothing) than a cynic. Cynicism ranks lowest on my scale of values.

During COVID (when I needed money), I stumbled into accepting a paid commission to edit a real estate financier's book on the crisis of trust in our society. Here was a case, late in life, where I again thought someone possessed the values he professed.

In chapter after chapter, he described truly harrowing episodes of suffering betrayal. He soon betrayed me, chiseling me out of part of our contracted terms. This had to occur. His betrayals, which he revisited on others, were due to the nature of his relationships, formed with people like him. This was the unspoken—and unrealized—lesson of his book. If you want to know someone, know his company.

I maintain sparse company today. Beyond my household, my social contacts are few—not nonexistent but few. I am close only to people who have suffered and who understand the rarity of true relationship. Only in such cases is help warranted, given, and understood.

Knowing one's company requires going beyond cultural expectancies. New Age centers have bilked me out of money, or tried to, and then played the card they are "struggling nonprofits." Nonprofit is an IRS term. The National Rifle Association and Church of Scientology are nonprofits.

Worse than stealing money is withholding it. Or making people chase it down. Nothing is more humiliating to the worker, artist, contractor, or tradesperson than having to run after money or other resources following a job well done. Theft is more honest than delay or evasion. Delay is theft of cowards.

* * *

I say this: how you deal with money is not only self but search. Not because money is "real" or of ultimate value. But because it is the medium of human interaction most visibly and palpably placed in our hands in the physical sphere. It is directly and unambiguously *experienced*.

If you want to know me, witness my conduct around money. All else is a matter of claimed intent and self-testimony. Money is calculable.

In the U.S., we somnambulantly note the holiday of Labor Day, intended to honor wage-earning people. I cannot find a single foundational text in the surviving history of religion and ethics that does not elevate to special status the question of fairness regarding how one treats working people. We have founded a secular religion on this matter: Marxism, which, like all religions, cyclically becomes its opposite.

My challenge is not asking how spirituality relates to money or vice versa. Rather, it is to treat money, in and of itself, as the medium of the search, ethical, spiritual, or both.

All of the money in my life is earned by me alone. "He travels the fastest who travels alone." I paid for college on student loans and I invested heavily during my years in corporate publishing. I received a grand sum of $500 as a parental wedding gift in my first marriage. And I appreciated it. During the grimmest years of my youth, we experienced barely concealed middle-class poverty that nearly resulted in losing our home. As I write these words, I support or co-support three people, in addition to myself. I write this to make the point that I occupy no position of special privilege, beyond the obvious, where money is concerned. Hence, I do not believe I am setting an excessive standard.

I say a lot more about money than time in this chapter. As noted, I am better with giving money than time. If I must answer for something, it is, perhaps, my hoarding of time. Let me be judged by it.

* * *

Western concepts of who to give to, and when to give, are shaped by Abrahamic tradition. I do not have to agree with an outlook to recognize its genius or greatness.

A twin tenet of Christianity—I mean not Christendom but the philosophy of Christ—is abundant grace and mercy.

These ideas have antecedents in Judaism, where they are more muted and conditioned.

I reject them.

Having covered what is yours to give—*time and money*—I further reckon that these things and their dispensation are subject to *affinity*.

I consider this a more honest antonym to general concepts of service or charity, which are, as a rule, philosophies that must remain silent. Also as a rule, they are rarely abided silently. They are still more rarely acted on in any intelligent and meaningful manner.

The few who abide and act would still do so under my outlook. But with the added benefit that the vast majority, who neither abide nor act (though they talk), would have fewer hiding places. Truth is astringent.

I have an out-of-touch friend who many years ago gave a mutual friend $50,000 to help a sick family member. He rarely, if ever, spoke of it. I know of it privately. I admire it immensely. He is a Christian, or so I think. He would have done it if he worshiped Jupiter. Or Satan. *Because it arose from fineness of being and affinity*—and nothing else.

Fineness of being and affinity engender effortless reciprocity. The state I describe is emotional in nature and ethical in expression. It cannot be taught or enforced. It can be levied, which is fair game in terms of social policy. That is not my topic.

* * *

The morning of writing these words, I was in a doctor's office filled with people in need. I saw a young woman receiving an IV blood treatment. She sat in her recliner with a notebook and at one point slipped off her loafers, one of which unintendedly hit the tile floor with a thud. We made eye contact and laughed. The contrast between her and others in the wing, none in any more obvious position of fortune, resounded. That is someone I wish to help. I see my ideals in her, if not my habits of behavior.

Would you leave others to die? I anticipate that comment like the chime of a clock.

No. You would.

Ethics, solidarity, and reciprocity are not a sport or position. Helping or withholding are not polarities. Nor is one better than the other. Without awareness, both are near-meaningless. With awareness, both are vivifying.

A few among us, it could be argued, act from a sense of general good. They help strangers, including populations. In extreme situations—which are, by definition, rare—that impulse exists. That person, and I for that matter, attempt, however slightly and fragmentarily, to repair what is upended, which, too, is the impulse of fineness.

* * *

I know a historian who calls himself a "tribalist." It is not a term I use. I understand what he is driving at—he is signaling some kind of group, or presumably ethnic, solidarity. I grasp that and do not challenge it. But if I have such affinities, they are certainly not organized by nationhood, or not wholly. They are organized by recognition of shared fineness. Do I mean superiority? In honesty, yes.

Abiding, sustaining, and cultivating beauty—including the beauty of another person's aspirations and potential—is superiority.

"You think you're fucking better than them?" someone once demanded, as I foolishly winced over a crowd of *hoi polloi* (what other crowd is there?). The inability to allow another person to hold his or her own space is an inferior, or common, position from which to live. I was foolish because I was stepping into that space among the many, even as I demand it for the few.

Let me be clear about this. Abiding another's capacity for selfhood is exactly what I mean by personal fineness—and personal betterness.

Many have observed, rightly I think, how difficult it is to attend live events that do not feature booming distractions. Because few audience members are capable of allowing others to hold their own experience. They check their phones, talk at quiet moments, sing along, conduct in the air with their fingers, kick the back of someone's seat—anything but leave others alone.

* * *

Sensitive people immediately know and recognize one another. I have felt that truth literally everywhere I have lived or been, throughout the world, from my earliest retained memories.

Some reading this know exactly what I mean. Some will feel relief and recognition upon reading it. You are not alone. You are, however, isolated.

I often tell people that it is better to be nobly alone or isolated than to settle for an abundance of low company, which depletes and reduces you. I consider this literally true.

I was talking recently with an artist who designs fine jewelry. She is impeccable. She was telling me about routinely visiting New York's diamond district in Midtown Manhattan, a place that I had ironically just returned from. If you have never visited it, my advice is: don't.

I nodded in silent sympathy as she described how the experience produced unease in her for days after, even sometimes the night before. This is not imaginary and it is not metaphorical. I do not know what "energy" is—it is an overused term. But it exists, and one can feel its depletion chemically, though more than that alone.

Protect yourself from this. Exclude yourself from the wrong kinds of Thanksgiving dinners and funerals. The consequences will pale compared to what you gain.

As an adolescent, I complained to a close family member that most of our relatives seemed to me assholes. They lacked generosity and rarely lent a hand to neighbors, friends, or passersby, even if asked. They were cheap.

"That's the immigrant mentality," came the answer. But they were not immigrants. Their parents were. Environment did not make them coarse. Being made them coarse. I recall one exception. Her life is notable because it differed in no visible way—not looks, money, circumstance—from anyone else's.

Recent to this writing, I saw the movie *Marty Supreme*. It made me almost physically ill, not because it is bad but great. The filmmaker's depiction of his "supreme" hero features relatives and from-the-neighborhood types who are too real for me. Marty's position apropos of them is glaringly clear.

The notion that we are all born in grace, or born in sin as a station from which to achieve grace, rings false to me. I cannot verify it. Empathy, temperament, character—all inchoate terms—appear from infancy. Any sensitive parent (I have two grown sons) knows this. Barring extremes, environment can move the individual's dial a few degrees one way or another. But rarely and temporarily.

I say: the only people due your help, engagement, assistance, and even empathy are those who make you feel less alone—those whom you know not by forensics but shared selfhood.

Won't the world go the hell if we speak this—and live it? We already live it, more or less. So things will get no worse.

I believe: they will get better. Because luminosity averts injury and provides clarity.

If you disdain what I have written, wait twenty-four hours. Is your search, by which I mean your life, worth twenty-four hours? See if my statement does not more clearly organize who you are and what you owe.

We all sustain debt for our existence. Start paying it now. Start sincerely. That which begins sincerely continues.

SEVEN

What Is Power?

I write from life. I must assume that no life is exclusive. Hence, when I draw conclusions—I write on the eve of my sixtieth birthday—about life on the path, I think they hold something for you.

I immediately cringe at my opening gambit: here comes another *life is this* or *life is that*—hoary wisdom that C.S. Lewis or some other eminence has already stated better. I am, of course, not a runner-up to such figures. My path is my own. It has consisted, and continues to consist, of the search for power. I contend this is everyone's path, clothed in different terms and insistencies.

Have I found power? I have not.

Power is agentic. It is limited by physicality, accident, and circumstance. It is stymied by the disparate pieces in which we find ourselves—mental, emotional, physical, sexual.

To speak of awakening, enlightenment, self-realization, or self-mastery is delusion. Such statements assume control that does not exist in any practical sense. I wrote a book called *Secrets of Self-Mastery*. I like the book—but hate the title.

That said, life conforms in measure to mental or psychical causation.* The fruits of that causation reach you through channels that may appear ordinary—and disregardable—or that may arrive in unusual ways. But the arc exists.

Return, right now, to your earliest retained memories and see if you do not agree. We may impose patterns after the fact. But not always.

We are imprisoned by emotion. Patterns of unmet needs and old scars enclose us for a lifetime. The situation is, I venture, not a problem—because it is without solution. A horse is startled by a harmless noise. It is innate to life. Save your money on the shrink.

Again my principle: what a thirsty person needs is not a statement on water—but water. I believe that the search—for truth, extra-physicality, ethics, meaning—is enacted on the playing field of quotidian life. Not somewhere outside of it. If you need more money, as nearly everyone reading these words does, devise ways

* I sometimes reference causation in this book. That is a deliberate framing. The causation-correlation debate in science is active and meaningful. I use causal language in a practical, observational sense.

of finding money. That exchange, necessary and vital, is as much a part of the search as the act of meditation. Perhaps more so.

People complain that Transcendental Meditation costs too much. Shortly before his death in 2008, Maharishi Mahesh Yogi remarked to a friend of a friend, "People will have no idea what we were trying to accomplish here." I take that as truth.

I do not wish to drag truth into absolute literalness, especially since it has many dimensions. But I will add that paying for meditation—and what it summons from within you (e.g., enterprise, complaint)—may be as self-elucidating as the act itself. That is a fragment of Maharishi's allusion.

A friend, Bob Roth, is executive director of the David Lynch Foundation, which teaches Transcendental Meditation. Bobby learned to meditate from Maharishi. Learning from him is a privilege.

He told me a story, which I repeat from memory:

> People sometimes complain to me that learning TM is too expensive. I tell them to write me a letter explaining why they want to learn—and I will teach them free. Not one in ten people write that letter.

Of course not. Because they do not wish to meditate. They wish to complain. That is why social media is how it is. You have a different relationship to the things you pay for.

If you want to see how little people value things, give them something unearned such as a promotion, access to a valuable person, or placement on a team or project populated by others who have labored long and hard to get there. They will not aspire to prove themselves. They will not seek mentors. They will demand more. And then launch into fury when not granted it.

Gurdjieff used to say that when you help someone, they first fall to their knees thanking you; then they require more; then they sue you. This is absolute truth.

I observe this in Hollywood, a high-risk, high-reward environment that seems to rob people of what little sense they possess to begin with, me included. Everyone—without exception—who works in screen, a tough world on its best day, has stories of the amateur who blew up a project. Such episodes could fill volumes. They are always the same: someone got lucky, was promoted beyond experience, and proceeded to tear down a project, damning everyone involved. Gurdjieff should have been an agent.

As an aside, here is my advice to those working in such environments. My teacher gave it to me. I have failed to embrace it. Maybe someone reading this will. *Use your intellect not your passions.*

Recent to this writing, someone who considers himself a martial artist and Freemason, fields that teach rank and honor, asked me to lunch. I accepted at my inconvenience. I did so cheerfully because I considered him a seeker.

I agreed to meet him at an out-of-the-way location, for me, because I, too, once held a day job, and I understand people's financial pressures. I had to reschedule and wrote a gracious note—because I value another's time. Our rescheduled lunch required me to ask a film crew to visit my home for a scouting session earlier than ideal, for them and my family.

I advertised none of this. Why would I? It is easily estimated.

Next, it was his turn to reschedule. Fair enough.

He wrote curtly, "Something came up." And offered me something about when his calendar would reopen.

That is human nature: obliviousness of debt, impact, and what has been granted. This is why Gurdjieff threw out letters requesting advice but without significant contributions. And why you should too. Even if I cannot. I am trying.

I worry that the search, or what we conceive of it, functions as a consolation. This is not a sincere motive. The search is not a booby prize. I think it is better and nobler to fail at life than to tell yourself life's goodies aren't so valuable after all, hence I will study Buddhism. You can neither sacrifice, nor stand in judgment over, what you have not attained.

That said, the playing field of attainment must be carefully selected. I got an email the other day from an associate producer who asked me to audition for a franchise show with which I have significant history. He did not know. It was a template letter. I think the field of screen work may be a bad place for me. I haven't the emotional armor for it. Note this in selecting a road.

Relationships are the core facet of life. They govern power. We sustain too many. And so squander power. If, as I have suggested, people are like horses, easily startled and requiring managing, how many horses do you want to consort with? Think of how much pain follows you in life due to unnecessary relationships. Do you wish to change your life? Start there.

Recent to this writing, someone complained over social media that my writing on Neville Goddard and his philosophy of mind creation induced him into a crisis of debt-spending. I made the dubious decision to respond. I harbor critical and subtle sympathy for

Neville, an intellectual hero to me. This prompted the usual hyperbolic thread responses and I quickly exited.

I make my personal email available on my website. I have reproduced it on social media. I offer it to anyone who has an issue with something I have said or written, as I did in this case. The email went unused. It is never used by complainers. Because they have no real argument with my ideas. *Here I am—write me.* They do not want that. They want to condemn—for theater and attention.

In any case, I felt a deficit of purpose. I offered engagement and it ended in superficial rejoinder. My vulnerability led me to a question that many people, in many variants, ask themselves: What is my right seat of selfhood, expression, and—without sentimentality—personal power?

The Vedic traditions are historically hierarchical. Hindu lore holds that the Vedas, the ancient expression of arts, sciences, family, sexuality, social order, world cycles, and spiritual insight, emerged from early India's Brahmin families. From this primeval framing emerged an archly stratified caste order.

Depending on viewpoint, this caste order reflects either the natural harmony of a spiritual polity or a drearily oppressive and burdensome social anachronism. My best reckoning is that absolute truth lies in neither polarity.

I observed a social dynamic of this type—vastly different but not wholly unrelated—in the Gurdjieff work. Those who found their way in that work required an almost-organic or innate sensibility of who belonged in charge. Following a dinner after a day of group work, my teacher, now deceased, said: "The senior people may speak. And by senior, I mean those who are always willing to give."

My teacher, as I saw it, was always willing to give. His efforts were endless. I once heard a colleague whisper to herself, "Oh Jon, thank you for all you give."

That said, other colleagues, some older than me, resented him. They viewed him as a barrier to their own expression and advancement in the work. "The greatest barrier to the work," he once told me, "is ambition in the work."

Was he right? I warrant he was. But ambition differs from understanding. I encountered people in the work who could not see, and hence could not respect, those who had surpassed their level of understanding. This surpassing was sometimes a matter of fineness of emotions and insight. Sometimes it was a matter of effort. Often all of these. To oppose failure to see this opposition is internal—is not ambition.

There occur times in outer life—and this is a key to worldly success, so mind it carefully—when you must understand whose place it is to talk and to give directions, if any are needed. Recall Sarah Orne Jewett's heroine Betty: "no two persons can be placed anywhere where one will not be host and the other guest. One will be in position to give and to help and to show; the other must be the one who depends and receives." I know people who derailed their careers by not realizing whose turn it was to talk or act. My wife Jacqueline Castel is a feature film director. Her manager once told her: "The thing I like about you is, you always know who you are talking to." There is power in that.

Here is what I am driving at. Power, in its natural sense, is not exactly money, possessions, connections, intellect, lineage, looks, or inheritance—although none of those things can possibly be discounted in our world. Power is, rather, understanding fineness of being and what it requires from self and others. This fineness of being may vary based upon requirements of a situation. That said, it is not conditional. When real, it exists always and everywhere.

An expression appears in different spiritual traditions from Taoist to Talmudic. I put it this way: "Know ten things, speak nine." Within that is power. Speaking or acting beyond one's place is weakness. So is speaking or acting below one's place. That was my sin described earlier.

Secret of Oedipus

Fear of losing power, or of inadequately measuring up to it, leads to over-compensation, which is the surest way of losing power. That is the secret of the self-fulfilling prophecy of Oedipus, as described in Sophocles' tragedy.

We all witness self-fulfilling prophecies in which we or others trigger the thing most feared. But why? Why should fear alone produce an event? Do we psychically "attract" it? Do we precognitively sense it? Or something else?

As I pondered the nature of self-fulfilling prophecies it came to me that, again and again, the decisive factor is overcompensation. Overcompensation is one of our greatest adversaries. Fear of rejection, for example, may result in forcing yourself on someone, which inevitably summons rejection. We overcompensate for perceived flaws. And, hence, we bring those flaws, phantom or not, to the pinnacle of our lives. It is a strange symmetry.

But unrealized power dwells within that symmetry—provided we can become aware of it. If events are self-created, they may be self-altered.

The doomed hero Oedipus self-fulfilled the prophecy that he would kill his father and wed his mother. In the events of *Oedipus Rex*, the protagonist—powerful in intellect but vulnerable in pride and easily provoked to anger—is so fearful of this prophecy that he summons it through a series of rash behaviors.

Fear of outcome, when extreme, engenders behaviors that are intended as medicine but instead are poison. It is observed that medicine and poison are the same, depending upon dose.

Hence, someone who fears exclusion, either in business, friendship, or intimacy, often copes with that fear by acting out in ways that make his or her exclusion a fact. There may, on occasion, be a kernel of truth to one's fears. But exaggeration or lack of self-awareness make that kernel a far greater factor than is necessary.

Overcompensation also blinds us—Oedipus ultimately suffers blindness—so that we fail to detect the opportunity to bypass wrong situations or company in favor of something more promising.

Before moving on to an example, let me share a secret with you. If you value it, the returns will prove extraordinary. In an unpublished talk, Napoleon Hill (1883–1970) cautioned: "Avoid persons and circumstances which make you feel inferior."

I return to the question of over-compensation. To cite a small but vivid example, I watched this play out in a mini psychodrama at a party one night. An out-of-town guest was eager to be seen and heard. He kept insistently butting into conversations or interrupting people. He wanted their acceptance, company, and recognition. But his anxiety to be seen made the same people whose attention he sought distance themselves. It is a template of what I am describing.

Ask yourself today: What am I summoning? Do I really want it? And, if so, why? If not, why not? Pay less attention, for now, to the motive behind your desire than to what your desire is delivering. I personally believe we over-dwell, often fruitlessly, on motive. Motive can prove mysterious and contradictory. *Watch for what is delivered.*

And if the event, or more likely the pattern of events, causes you pain, is it actually a misdirected search for selfhood and power?

We often receive what we seek. And seek what we desire. What is sought may cause suffering—but it also delivers something, albeit through a self-negating form of attention or the uneasy relief of self-compelled failure. We sometimes impel failure to cope with its perceived inevitability. Watch for these factors.

And when you find yourself in situations that seem to beckon overcompensation, exit immediately. You are in the wrong place to exercise natural power and you will deplete what you possess.

* * *

Observation is the tool on which discernment rests. Not just any observation but a special sort. Intellect is part of observation, as are emotions and body. But intellect moves slowly. Emotions and body steal its energy. When my teacher met a newcomer, he would often look that person up and down. Slowly. Like a dog does. He knew.

Humanity is broken in such a way that interrupts this natural cycle of observation. I do not know how to restore it. It may not be restorable. But I do believe that where there appears a lock, somewhere must be a key. We have lost the key. We look for the key in obvious places, not because it is there but because such places are better lit. That is a mistake.

Commerce is a measure of power, as is stardom, ownership, invention, strength, and sexuality. But all of these, while authentic, are incomplete.

Power emerges only from a moment of fineness of self when observation is felt throughout one's being: intellectual, emotional, physical. When those rare moments occur, you will know—and fleetingly understand—power.

People used to share copies of a book called *Tuesdays with Morrie*, a "meaning of life" book. I knew the literary agent. When I was a kid editor, age twenty-five, he insulted me across a lunch table in a restaurant. I was so taken aback I thought of leaving and regret having not. There may be more truth in that encounter than in the book. Within this choice—although emotions took it from me—lies power. Protect yourself in life. Never consort with fools or suffer them. Into that gap steps power.

Power is relational. Its moments will pass. They cannot be summoned again at will. They become story or memory, as the case for me in writing these words and for you in reading them. But that power occurs—when relations are rightly aligned—means that it is real. And also that somewhere lies the key. It may appear for you in the next chapter.

EIGHT

Dignity

We often approach spirituality, like therapy, to salve a crisis of poor self-image. This is not to be fled or denied but embraced.

I will never forget the painful experience at age twelve of writing in a diary, long-since discarded, *"I am cool!"* This impotent adolescent plea, its assertion belying the claim, follows us into adulthood.

The term "cool" dominates our vernacular, though it is probably losing primacy in the lexicon.

What does it even mean?

It means: *self-sustaining.*

Coolness is not inextricably bound to fashion, looks, mannerisms, appearance, or risk-taking, though all of these have value. Popular media, starting in the mid-twentieth century, defined coolness by these traits in the same manner that Disney's *Snow White* rendered us incapable of seeing in our mind's eye anything other than the brunette animated princess when the centuries-old myth is evoked.

Back of coolness is another, older concept: dignity, from Latin *dignus* or *worthy.*

That—and that alone—*dignity,* is what my twelve-year-old self sought. And what you seek. I know because no life is exclusive.

* * *

I often write about the possibilities of mind causation or what is popularly, though inadequately, called *manifesting.* I am rethinking my opposition to it. "A rose by any other name." Why quibble over terms?

Whatever I decide, I abide a model of radical idealism in which the thought-forms of the psyche do, in fact, *select* elements of experience, and concretely so.

Some highbrows deride what I describe as solipsism. They are wrong. The difference between the solipsist and the idealist is that the former imposes on others to prop up his self-image. This is why people find it more satisfying to argue over social media than via private exchange. They can achieve more in private. But that is secondary. The prize is not ideas but attention.

Summoning another to affirm my self-image is yelling into a cracked mirror. It is not only ineffective but eroding of dignity.

* * *

Only a person stripped of dignity understands its nature.

I once knew someone who lived in a modular home, in which she raised two sons. I admired her. Her mother, in front of the boys, called it "a trailer."

"It's not a trailer," she said. Her mother already knew that. What's more, she knew the implication of her statement.

I cannot tell another person what to do. But—if it were me—I would sever ties with such a person. Consequences be damned.

There are, of course, other roads. If the consequences seem too great, and this can change over time, and if you can find within yourself a place of containment—an underground spring of value—you have retained dignity.

Where is this "underground spring"? Does it exist? Not in assertions made from one's couch—but really?

It must exist. I experience it, for example, when practicing Transcendental Meditation, which I personally consider an accelerant to that place. Such a spring exists and is findable in other ways.

For example, the day you separate from cruelty, you have found it. The moment of a shock—arising from grief or euphoria—when conditioned responses cease (and will inevitably return), you have found it. Those who undergo conversion experiences, in which a moment of clarity objectively reorganizes outer circumstance, have found it. When you pay a debt, broadly defined, you have found it.

* * *

The experience I describe cannot always be summoned. That is a rule. But there exist interim steps that help cultivate access to this inner spring, the source of dignity.

Chief among them: *know what you really want*. You may not always be capable of attaining it; but, in matters large and small, really know. And acknowledge it.

Another way is desisting from trash talk and gossip, which erode and pollute inlets from the inner spring. Such talk exchanges the dopamine-hit thrill of degrading another for the sustenance of rightness. This is the esoteric meaning of Esau selling his birthright for a bowl of pottage.

Speak as you must—but remember that *speech dilutes* and speech that demeans another redounds to self in the form of decay. This is the law of reciprocity. You cannot visit emotional violence on another without debt. The surest way that debt is taken—*and nature will take it*—is from your own skin.

The depletion you feel in self-betrayal drives you back to the prior place of excitement—of defaming another—and the cycle of self-destruction continues.

If you doubt me, give one hour to desisting from any talk or posting that demeans another. Track the results. Is your existence worth an hour?

* * *

Over-compensation for perceived (and possibly real) flaws destroys dignity. Remember, Oedipus was ruined not due to prophecy—wedding mother and killing father—but due to determination to avert it. Aversion to circumstance decimated him: it created the circumstance.

I do not advocate acceptance. I am not a stoic, I am not a Christian, and I am not in pursuit of non-attachment. Popular iterations of those outlooks often tear the seeker in two.

Rather, I look for a path. My own path. I wander from it. I get lost. I fail. I know when those things occur because they always involve *taking from another person*. Or pleading for something, such as approval, which someone may not wish to give.

* * *

I have been in professional settings where I felt constantly angry—deprived of the respect and authority

I felt due. I was not imagining things. Nor are you. In such cases, the problems are real enough. For example, I may have felt obligated toward mediocre people. But I remained. I tolerated. I allowed contact. In that respect, the problem was less setting than self.

Should I—or you—leave? In a word, yes. But if that proves temporarily impossible or too grave in consequence, return to what I suggested earlier: know your preferences, acknowledge them—and vow, internally and privately, to act on them at the nearest physical opportunity.

If done sincerely, you will experience restored dignity, or self-sustenance. That is the place of true worth. That is the "coolness" for which I yearned in youth.

Individuals can endure a great deal of sorrow. They cannot endure compromise of dignity. Because they do not know this, they flee indignity through all kinds of self-negating behaviors, such as smiling at a bully or going along with events from which they recoil or complaining incessantly.

These become desperate efforts that, as Oedipus did, summon the hated thing.

I say: if you face circumstances that present a choice between isolation and indignity, seize the former. Be nobly alone, if you must. See what you find.

Within your seeming isolation you will, in effect, live off the land, i.e., seek sustenance from the resources available. That will finally drive you to the inner spring I reference. Its waters, like those of the fabled fountain of Bethesda, bring healing—in the form of dignity: self-sustainment.

* * *

In his 1841 lecture "Man the Reformer," Ralph Waldo Emerson (1803–1882) asked: "Can we not learn the lesson of self-help? Society is full of infirm people, who incessantly summon others to serve them."

Emerson was referring not to the destitute but rather those who clamor for life's niceties while producing little.

By contrast, Emerson asked: "Can anything be so elegant as to have few wants and to serve them one's self, so as to have somewhat left to give, instead of being always prompt to grab?"

Pursuing this ideal of "self-help"—Emerson coined the term in his lecture—does not require personal crisis, addiction, or heralding some thunderous change in your life. It can begin, and in some regards must, in subtly and quietly self-determined ways.

This, by the way, gives you an idea of why many humanities academics and legacy critics detest Emerson as a sentimental myth-maker. Because he undermines the role that theorists often religiously ascribe to working people—i.e., working people in their imagination not in actuality, where they rarely know them, as I do. So do many of you. People with easy resources rarely read my stuff.

* * *

I never met twentieth-century spiritual teacher Vernon Howard but I am influenced by his outlook and directness. He observed that we automatically, often by default, burden others with our needs, creating a cycle of dependency that expands throughout our lives. This cycle also fosters resentment in others even if they never let on.

To interrupt this cycle, Vernon said, start by doing small things for yourself.

For example, when you are at home, instead of bothering someone else with a question about where a household object can be located—such as tape or scissors—take it upon yourself to search for the object, which is almost always findable. Only if a search fails to turn it up should you ask another, "Do you know where the scissors are?"

You will be surprised at how rarely you even need to ask help from another, and thus place a needless claim on his or her time. Make it a practice.

Do you want to carry your own load through life or rely upon others to carry it?

Do not respond too quickly to that question. I have stumbled in life because I liked the idea—however much I concealed it from myself at the time—of making *someone else responsible for carrying my load* in one way or another.

Overly depending on others erodes your self-respect as it also erodes your abilities and acumen. Try doing as much for yourself as possible in small situations and consider how this reverberates through larger and more consequential areas of life.

This does not mean that you will not need to ask help. But the ask should come only *after* you've made every reasonable effort to unclog a toilet, locate a tool, install or remove an air conditioner, plaster a crack, or mount a picture. Even if you do so imperfectly you will have won a victory. You will sense it. So will others, even if indirectly. In time, such actions will improve your relationships and self-respect.

Years ago I volunteered to perform ten days of trail maintenance on the Appalachian Mountains in New York State. The other volunteers and I dug drainage channels, blazed trees, cleared brush and branches, and set or reset natural boundaries. It was grueling labor in mid-summer heat. I loved every minute and never slept better.

About halfway through the experience, however, one of the younger volunteers grew desultory. She began asking others—at mealtime, on the trail, during labor—to find things for her, hand things to her, and perform small tasks that were easily within her reach. Resentment began to simmer. Good thing we weren't in a lifeboat.

Speaking of which: How would you be regarded in a lifeboat? That is your lived philosophy.

The events I describe occur routinely in life: *people rarely express it* but this dynamic foments subliminal tension that prevails in many households and workplaces. The cycle can be disrupted, if not broken, by displaying self-sufficiency in small ways. This, too, feeds dignity.

NINE

Do You Enjoy Suffering?

I challenge spiritual settings or voices that seek to rearrange or spin around cries for happiness, as though satisfaction with self and surroundings is a misdirected or abrogated plea from a "lesser I." The problem with happiness is not its destination but the clarity with which it is sought.

In that vein, the greatest barrier to your happiness is the *secret pleasure that you derive from suffering.*

Does that sound absurd or affected? It is not.

Human beings are generally selfish. When you repeat something over and over there is usually a principle of self-gain present even in areas that appear fraught with pain.

Grenade Pins

I had a close family member who constantly—even in the midst of good times and, it seemed, especially in the midst of them—would emotionally pull grenade pins. She would do things that could only and inevitably cause arguments and hurt feelings. I witnessed this behavior during or immediately following family gatherings that were otherwise marked by comity and relative peace. It was a pattern.

With predictability, either during a social event or the next day, she would blow things up with an inappropriate remark or gratuitous demand. I often tried to speak with her about this to elucidate and ameliorate the pattern. But to no avail. At such times, she would profess no understanding of what I was describing. After years of fruitless communication, it finally occurred to me: this person was enjoying what was going on. She found conflict thrilling and empowering.

Vernon Howard called this "a false feeling of life." It is related to the sensation one gets when viewing violence, firing a gun, or posting a bilious comment. It can be addictive. And devastatingly fractious when applied to relationships.

The person I describe was a family intimate—but damn me if I am not equally self-probing. I wrestle with anxiety, which is projected fear. It is, by nature, anticipatory. Ostensibly, I do not "enjoy" feeling afraid. And yet . . . even though the effects of fear may include pain, the emotion itself—much like anger, aggression, truculence, intimidation, or cries of victimhood—often delivers a kind of thrill. It provides relief from the routines of life. It makes me feel as though I am the center of attention. If not for a payoff, why else persist in clearly hurtful patterns?

It has been observed that even unhappy familiarity holds a reassuring quality, such as painful family dynamics. I have heard the term "trauma bonding." I honor that. But my proposition is based on slightly different premises.

Vernon once asked students to write the phrase "false feeling of life" on a slip of paper—and then study it for six months. We crave reward—this "false feeling of life" or thrill—but we often deny the negative manner through which we seek it.

The feeling of a thrill—so evident from gladiatorial events in antiquity and violent sports media and gaming today (along with much more)—is constantly sought. Watch carefully for whether you gain a sense of contest, aliveness, or thrill, through what is called suffering, either through witnessing, inflicting, or self-inflicting it.

It is rarely easy for me to observe this pattern in my own life. But my contention—and I am working on this with you as I write these words—is that what is found is generally what is sought. This is true even when the thing sought reaches us in a form we complain about.

Sometimes complaining is the point. Watch for whether your burdens are self-selected as a means to attention, thrill, solicitation of help, relief of boredom, or some other payoff. And if the event, or more likely the pattern of events, causes you pain, is it actually a misdirected search for selfhood and power?

"Why Me?" Is a False Question

What I am describing is not always easy to sort out. The body feels an emotion and the mind rushes in with a reason why. Yet the emotion is already present. Hence, the "reason" is often secondary. We tend to assign reasons after the fact of emotions.

For all that, I have responsibility for my repetitive returns to thoughts and figments aligned to fear. I cleave to certain patterns, people, or situations. Self-responsibility is undeniable.

So, rather than asking "why me?" I propose you ask: "What do I gain from this? Am I enjoying my suffering?"

As alluded, the seemingly self-defeating act of the same negative ritual must deliver gain. My family member liked conflict. I came to accept that. For my part, I, too, like suffering or inner conflict. It provides a kind of visceral thrill.

I cannot imagine that my experience is exceptional. None of us is as different from one another as we think. I ask you to search for the same pattern within.

Painful Reward

The greatest barrier you face to liberation—not the only, but the greatest—may be the thrill or pleasure you experience from a sense of victimhood, danger, unhappiness, or hopelessness.

This is no idle statement. For some reading this, it is your life.

I realize that circumstances are forced upon you, including parentage, health, physicality, geography, and economics. Where and in what circumstances you are born are a gravitational force. At the same time you also possess great latitude—which most of us routinely deny—regarding psychological choices and resources.

Take this day to face that in yourself.

It is often said—and I believe it true—that no one would be drug or alcohol addicted if it weren't enjoyable. Intoxication relieves stress. It creates temporary feelings of enthusiasm, conviviality, and euphoria.

Taken to dangerous excess, drugs and booze disrupt sleep patterns, promote lethargy and depression (which in turn requires higher doses), and eventually worsen everything they are ingested to escape.

Chronically negative, conflictual, or violent emotional reactions do the same thing. They actually feel good and thrilling at first—catch yourself in this. Be watchful. But the resulting enjoyment, which may arrive as a sudden rush of satisfaction or rightness, soon devolves into depression, panic, or deeper shades of anxiety. Hence, you must re-up the same "drug" to relieve its after-effects. This feeds caustic social media posts, as well.

If you can glimpse this even once in yourself, this observation of self—unadorned, unsentimental, and unindulgent—will open an entirely new door to you.

Shatter the Vessel

I must address one more form of stupid suffering—by which I mean suffering without awareness and, hence, reward and refinement. It is tolerating low company. And feeling oneself obligated to function within the values of low company—at which you constantly fail. If you take one thing from this book, make it this: shatter such settings and leave them. At the risk of sounding dramatic, this one move may save your life.

* * *

One night many years ago, I was having dinner alone at a restaurant on Manhattan's Upper West Side. Without intending to eavesdrop, I overheard two women at an adjacent table. They were clearly longtime friends, sharing what seemed a familiar, comfortable meal. But suddenly one of them said through tears: "You are so mean to me." Her companion replied, "I don't know what you're talking about."

This exchange, I later realized, reflects an unspoken crisis that touches nearly all human relations: cruelty.

If you are in proximity to people who diminish you, make you feel inferior, make subtle jokes at your expense, devalue your efforts or aims, deliver backhanded compliments, pretend to forget your job, or what you said five minutes earlier—whatever it is such people do to reduce you—I can say assuredly: you are not imagining things. Although your antagonists will assert that you are. *Plausible denial* is the chief tool of bullies or purveyors of cruelty.

As I noted at the outset: our culture is staggering under stress—and a good deal of it, I believe, emerges from the silently abided agony of relationships, random or close, family or professional, intimate or distant, longtime or new, steeped in cruelty. This crisis endures because it is unidentified—or when it is identified, its nature is watered down and effectively denied.

Nor are workable solutions presented. I believe that far too much is made of forgiveness, acceptance, or methods of verbal jujitsu within our spiritual and therapeutic cultures.

Even as therapeutic language and concepts abound, cruelty ranks among the least discussed aspects of human relations, albeit we sometimes categorize it (with fairness) under narcissism. Nonetheless, the problem of cruelty is often explained away or layered over with discursive and indirect approaches that burden the subject with fixing things. All is discussed except the one solution that actually and perennially works: getting away from cruelty without compromise.

We are taught to consider this solution last, if at all, and even then to over-ponder its consequences. And there are consequences. But usually of a far-lesser pitch than imagined. Think of it: escape is as close and as real as the words you are now reading. Act on this and your life, happiness, and sense of self will improve dramatically. You may rediscover yourself as a person of conviviality and relaxedness. This works when nothing else does. I vow from experience.

Read the following words carefully. *When you identify cruel people, never confront them or tell them you see through them.* They will only twist your claims against you, as did the interlocutor in my story above ("what do you mean? . . . you're too sensitive . . . I'm only joking . . . logically, what I said was . . . I have every right . . ."). The point is not to engage and get wounded again—it is to separate.

Cruelty and hostility run riot in social circles because antagonists enjoy it—and victims accept it. But this is not a requirement of life. As I noted in the meditation on power, we sustain too many relationships. If you factor in social media (itself a rampant source of cruelty), we probably encounter more people in a day than our ancient ancestors did in a lifetime.

It is vital, first and foremost, to physically separate from cruel, bullying, or depleting people. No amount of self-acceptance, acceptance of others, or verbal skill will build immunity to a relative, parent, boss, coworker, or "friend" who makes sport of running you down or who chronically directs subtle barbs at you.

It is all the more difficult when "stealth missiles" are fired at you in settings of ostensive relaxation, like dinners, outings, or parties. Subtle insults take you off guard and leave you nursing "woulda-shoulda" regrets of what might have been said. This is a waste of energy. Emotion is faster than intellect and more powerful. You are overwhelmed and stymied when insulted unexpectedly or subtly. This is a universal problem. More important than analyzing or understanding cruelty or hostility, or your response to it, is separating from it.

You cannot survive sustained hostility nor should you be expected to. This is true inasmuch as a houseplant cannot survive absence of sunlight or water. Such conditions are unnatural and unnecessary. Questions of forgiveness, understanding, and acceptance, whether of self or another, can be explored after you have gotten to safe ground.

Earlier I quoted success author Napoleon Hill. He is controversial today. I continue to abide Hill's work, which most journalistic and academic gatekeepers, sans familiarity, detest. The reasons are simple. They detest the self-help project, which violates psychologized concepts of what working people are supposed to represent. In any case, Hill was a shrewd observer of human nature. Hence, take what you are about to read with deadly seriousness. In 1945, he wrote:

> One must remove himself from the range of influence of every person and every circumstance which has even a slight tendency to cause him to feel inferior or incapable of attaining the object of his purpose. Positive egos do not grow in negative environments. On this point there can be no excuse for a compromise, and failure to observe it will prove fatal to the chance of success.

* * *

Some people feel unable to separate from a cruel antagonist due to family ties or financial needs. I sympathize with that—and offer this three-part approach:

1. Be certain that the bonds you feel are actual and not artificial. Fear of disapproval is not a valid excuse for remaining in proximity to a cruel person. Just because someone will disapprove of your decision is not a real bind. Every decision carries consequences; the positive consequences of distancing from cruelty almost invariably outweigh the negative. Another's judgment must not deter you. If it does, that is self-created.
2. If you have determined that you authentically wish to separate but are financially or otherwise bound, vow first to separate from the person internally. Acknowledge to yourself their cruelty and admit its grotesque and destructive nature. Never tell the other person what you are doing or thinking. Silently abide your insight. Remember: cruel people always have plausible denial. It is part of how they maintain their hold on you. Just knowing this makes you more powerful.
3. Vow to separate from the offender as a physical fact at the soonest possible opportunity. This

opportunity will come, and probably sooner than you think. This is because effort sustains and fortifies growth. When you place yourself within the schema of effort, which these three steps are designed to do, opportunities for expansion and movement reach you. But the first and crucial step is determining that escape is what you really want.

* * *

Once you actually separate from cruelty, you will be amazed at how many other facets of your life improve. In many cases, you will rediscover yourself as a person of humor, even temper, approachability, and steadiness.

I have been astonished to observe how many problems attributed to character, trauma, dysfunction, or over-sensitivity (a charge that cruel people almost always use to control you) suddenly lift once you are in the right company.

I believe that our therapeutic culture—positive as it has been in many ways—has inculcated many of us with the myth that our problems perpetually follow us unless we resolve psychological root causes or embrace correct "strategies." That is true in some cases. But in many cases I believe that children and adults are simply and egregiously misplaced. They are in the wrong kinds of company where they may feel bullied, misunderstood, or disdained. An altered setting can work dramatic changes, both personally and professionally.

I have been in settings where I had neighbors who were inconsiderate or hostile. Where my every effort at rapprochement ended disappointingly. I used to own a lake house in Upstate New York. When I drove up and saw my neighbor's car in his driveway my stomach would tighten—and this was a place for relaxation!—because he perpetually encroached on my property with noise, errant fireworks, twenty-four-hour spotlights, crowds, a garish floating dock anchored in the middle of the lake, and a not-infrequent wisecrack. He was, in short, an asshole.

No effort, from spiritual affirmations to personal appeals to a high fence made much difference. There was one solution. Moving. When I finally moved I felt great. I had been in the wrong setting. I am mindful that moving or breaking ties is not always possible. I owned that house for fifteen years. I walked away at a loss. But I want you to understand that sometimes the only solution is using your feet.

If you absolutely cannot separate from someone at present, for reasons of economics, domesticity, or livelihood, revisit the three points earlier. Swear silently that you will first separate from this person as a fact within—tell neither them nor anyone else of your vow—and you will free yourself as a physical fact at the soonest possible opportunity.

In the face of cruelty, most of us behave like sheep. But have you ever really observed sheep? One kick from a sheep can break a grown-man's ribs. Your kick is your power. We consider this question further in the next chapter.

TEN

If You Must Fight, Fight to Win

Conflict is an indelible part of existence; for most of us, most of the time, this is emotional-legal-relational. But not always.

This is a treatise on fighting. I open it with self-exposing frankness. I do so because I disdain the habit in our spiritual culture of using everything—including the term warrior itself—as a metaphor. Life in translation is not life. Later in this book, I call for greater transparency among spiritual communicators. I will not sink to hypocrisy.

I am not a warrior. I have never, beyond sparring in a boxing gym, punched someone.

As a child, I was on the weak end of the scale. Hence, I got easily intimidated. I hated it. Once around age eleven or twelve, some asshole called me a faggot—a term I dislike writing. I curled my fist. I moved it toward his stomach. He flinched. I did not punch him. I should have. Not just for me but for everyone who has ever been called that slur.

In recent years, I avoid street escalations because I have too much to lose.

So, who am I to write this consideration? An interpreter. Admittedly. And also someone who acknowledges that not all conflict is physical. Yet to neglect the physical, or leave it unmentioned, is avoidant, feckless, and fake. That is why I open on a confessionary note.

At my age, I am not looking for fights. Although I have I few candidates in mind. They would be better off not meeting me. In any case, if you accept me as your flawed guide—not warrior but interpreter—you may learn something.

Given its posterity and vast range of translations, the ancient Chinese martial guide *The Art of War* is among the oldest and most widely read works of practical philosophy in history—*actually read*, I emphasize, due to its clarity, urgency, and concision.

I focus on this martial guide because all others are folded within it.

In the spirit of practicality, I both open and close my exploration not with dates, names, and definitions—

all of those duly appear—but with practical methods to winning conflicts. The principle of this chapter is: *If you must fight, fight to win.*

Twenty-three dictums appear at the close. Ideas work better when you know what is behind them. Hence, my historical exegeses also help you win. Do not skip them.

* * *

At its heart, *The Art of War* is a Taoist work: its key principle is to attain victory by joining with the natural order of things. That is the book's approach to conflict and friction as it is to restoration and maintenance of peace. I believe the book's outlook is distillable to five basic points:

1. The greatest warrior prevails without fighting; *preparation, advantage,* and *rightness* (or the Tao) make conflict unnecessary.
2. Beware the devastation of conflict: war should never be pursued lightly.
3. Be eminently watchful: know your enemy, know yourself, know your terrain. *Fight only when all three assure victory.*
4. When you strike, *concentrate fury and power at your enemy's weakest point.*
5. When conflict ends, quickly restore peace. Protracted conflict corrodes victor and vanquished alike.

Although *The Art of War* is written from an explicitly martial perspective, its five ideals are Taoism itself. They counsel the reader to function like nature, the legendary author's definition of *rightness*.

Life functions along lines of generativity and reproduction in all its expressions; but for nature to perpetuate itself there exist innate and necessary schisms, such as a forest fire clearing away old brush. If left untouched, the brush would eventually overrun and choke the forest.

Nature is neither spiteful nor protractive. It works by direct and unimpeded means. The forest fire first takes dead leaves, branches, and underbrush. It eventually abates. And life regenerates.

Animals are not spiteful. I never use animal as an epithet. I might use savage.

An oceanographer once told me: "Life is what planets do"—the ecosystem of a planet or solar system (gravity itself abets life) creates homeostasis. Seen in a certain light, that is an expression of the Tao, or Way.

There is no simple manner of identifying the author of *The Art of War.* Nor is it entirely clear that there existed a single author. The book is traditionally attributed to Zhou dynasty general Sun Tzu (c. 544–496 B.C.), an honorific title meaning Master Sun.

The hallowed warrior is said to have recorded his insights around 500 B.C., although some historians argue for a later date. Beyond parables, little is known about this commander and strategist who does not formally appear in ancient Chinese historical literature until soon after 100 B.C., four centuries following his recorded death.

In this sense, Sun Tzu is somewhat like Hellenic sage Pythagoras (c. 570–495 B.C.), with whom, if certain records are accepted, he shares contemporaneous ancestry, and whose life, like Master Sun's, is known from writings that followed the philosopher's death sometimes by centuries.

In the modern West, we are accustomed to view writing as the work of distinct authors with private insights. But that model did not necessarily prevail among early ancient philosophers and historians.

In both the East and West, the more common practice was for scribes—versus authors with fixed personas—to espouse the outlook of philosophical schools, military orders, governments, and religious castes. That is the process by which Scripture itself was written. Likewise the Vedas. Most primeval writers and sages, including Homer and Socrates, did not possess clearly demarcated historical identities. Consensus holds that such figures may have existed either as single personas or composites.

Hence, ambiguity of authorship is not oddity—but ancient norm. A case in point appears in how Renaissance scholars and translators marveled at the late-ancient Greek-Egyptian writings attributed to Hermes Trismegistus, or thrice-greatest Hermes, a Greek title for Egypt's god of intellect, Thoth.

Among Renaissance thinkers, Hermes Trismegistus was considered a psychopomp of great antiquity. Later scholarship, however, demonstrated that the writings attributed to Hermes, grouped under the umbrella of Hermetica, actually dated to the generations immediately following the death of Christ—not the mists of primeval history. The sagacious byline Hermes Trismegistus got appended to these works by multiple scribes who—in a common ancient practice—fixed the name of a mythical or honored figure to their work to lend it gravity or authority.

That practice is not, in itself, a mark of inauthenticity. Like Taoism in classical Chinese, Hermetic literature is likely a retention of very ancient oral tradition written down in expository Greek in the closing centuries of Ancient Egyptian civilization. Hence, the Hermetica, like *The Art of War*, is a vital expression of humanity's primeval insight, regardless of authorship.

In the history of ideas, it matters less who wrote *The Art of War*—if there was a single author—than the historical integrity of its verses. Indeed, the Taoist naturalism and deep antiquity of *The Art of War* make the short work perhaps the most enduring and widely read expression of ancient Chinese philosophy—or possibly any branch of philosophy—of all time.

Given the book's vast number of modern reproductions, search-engine results, and ubiquitous appeal, I venture that *The Art of War* is, in our era, more widely read than the similarly mysterious and almost certainly older work on whose insights it rests: the *Tao Te Ching*. Authorship of the *Tao* is attributed to mythical sixth-century B.C. sage Lao Tzu, another honorific meaning Old Master.

Of the two legendary sages—Lao Tzu and Sun Tzu—the general Master Sun seems to maintain greater hold on the public mind.

It is not difficult to understand why the descendant has more eyes on it than its ancestor. Although the *Tao Te Ching* soars on philosophical wings, *The Art of War*, at times similarly lyrical, gets straight down to business. Its aim is not, or not solely, naturalistic insight—but hardcore victory. For Master Sun, victory rests on brutal efficiency.

It behooves would-be warriors, however, to note the closing lines of the *Tao Te Ching*, which express an outlook at the core of Sun Tzu's point of view: "He who proceeds violently across the earth will die a weary death. Know this, and you know all my teachings."

The Art of War, as we experience it in translation (you just read one of mine), is a modern work. Its public history in the West is roughly traceable to 1772 when a Jesuit missionary to Peking, Father Jean Joseph Marie Amiot (1718–1793), published a French translation in Paris. The book was feted in the press. Speculation held that it was read by Napoleon himself.

It was not until 1905, however, that the work got translated into English by Captain Everard Ferguson Calthrop (1876–1915), a British naval officer stationed in Tokyo. History has not been kind to his effort. British Sinologist and translator Lionel Giles (1875–1958) wrote in the introduction to his far more widely read 1910 translation:

> Unfortunately, it was evident that the translator's knowledge of Chinese was far too scanty to fit him to grapple with the manifold difficulties of Sun Tzu. He himself plainly acknowledges that without the aid of two Japanese gentlemen "the accompanying translation would have been impossible." We can only wonder, then, that with their help it should have been so excessively bad.

Giles proved as enterprising as he was blunt. An assistant curator at the British Museum and caretaker of the Department of Oriental Manuscripts and Printed

Books, as well as the son of an influential British diplomat and Chinese linguist, Herbert Giles, the scholar produced his own painstaking, elegant, and enticingly spare translation of *The Art of War.*

Giles's sculpted and meticulous prose set the standard for nearly every translation that followed, of which there were dozens. Although new English translations arrive steadily—and there is always room for points of clarity and refinement, both textual and historical—none, in my reading, have surpassed the Zen-like precision of Giles's 1910 effort.

During World War II, Giles fatefully granted permission to The Military Service Publishing Company of Harrisburg, Pennsylvania, to issue his translation for military and general readers.

The 1944 volume is stripped of ancient Chinese characters as well as the translator's extensive footnotes, in which he expanded on language or textual points and sometimes added historical commentary. Yet I consider the wartime digest an immensely valuable effort that served to preserve, popularize, and familiarize the reading public with this vital work. Without it, *The Art of War* might not be as widely known today.

In my work, I attempt to follow Giles's considerable footsteps. I believe in ardent learning. I believe, too, in popular treatment. I loathe snobbery and affected seriousness.

I recommend reading Giles's translation of *The Art of War*—which I use here—in tandem with his 1905 translation of the *Tao Te Ching*, or, as he titled it, *The Sayings of Lao Tzu*. This relates to my earlier point: *The Art of War* stands on the shoulders of the *Tao Te Ching*. Reading them together fosters fuller understanding. (I edit an annotated joint edition.)

To summarize, the Tao, meaning roughly the Way, signifies the flow of nature. It is the underlying order of creation and the eternal cycle behind and through all things. Functioning within the Tao means functioning as a natural being—and, in the vision of Sun Tzu, a victorious warrior.

* * *

Why does any of this background matter? Is an ancient martial work and its Taoist antecedent really useful to contemporary readers? These works are useful—even urgent—on two counts: practical and ethical, although the two are one, another Taoist principle.

As Sun Tzu taught, there occur periods when friction or conflict inevitably crosses your path. In the Taoist view, this is not a rupture with nature but an expression of it.

When contention occurs, classical Chinese philosophy suggests, we face *five basic choices*, as we do in all general situations. The five choices are implied in the still-older Chinese oracular, calendric, and ethical work, the *I Ching* or *Book of Changes* (c. late ninth century B.C.). Its sixty-four hexagrams rank among the oldest writing in history. The five choices are:

1. Stop
2. Go back cautiously
3. Go back rapidly
4. Move ahead cautiously
5. Move ahead energetically

In the spirit of Taoist philosophy, none of these courses is better or more honorable than another. The only relevant question is: *which aligns with the Tao*?

In helping you reach that determination, *The Art of War* proves a wonder of practical wisdom. But the work suggests broader social implications.

British military historian Captain B. H. Liddell Hart (1895–1970), one of the clearest and canniest voices of military historicism of the twentieth century, observed in his foreword to a 1963 translation by Samuel B. Griffith:

> Civilization might have been spared much of the damage suffered in the world wars of this century if the influence of [Carl von] Clausewitz's monumental tomes *On War*, which moulded European military thought in the era preceding the First World War,

> had been blended with and balanced by a knowledge of Sun Tzu's exposition on "*The Art of War.*"

The martial philosophy of Prussian general and military strategist Clausewitz normalized war as an extension of state policy: "politics by other means," he put it. Clausewitz further taught that once war is undertaken it must be pursued to its absolute ends. The sole requisite of conflict, Clausewitz wrote, is using any and every means to annihilate the enemy.

For some post-war Western commanders, especially in the wake of America's defeat in Vietnam, Clausewitz's work reflected back-to-basics practicality and repudiation of political notions of waging "limited war"—a policy popularized in the era of Vietnam strategy. To Liddle Hart, however, the Prussian's endorsement of totalized warfare, and his tone of cold logic in pursuing destruction, contrasted poorly with Sun Tzu's "realism and moderation."

For Sun Tzu, war is not a neutral extension of politics; it is a grave and final resort whose risks must be mitigated. And—while raw victory is essential to Sun Tzu's doctrine—he posits restoration of normalcy as war's ultimate aim.

In terms that would have sounded off-key if not alien to Clausewitz and his disciples, Sun Tzu stresses thinking flexibly about objectives. For example, Sun

Tzu cautions: "Do not interfere with an army that is returning home. When you surround an army, leave an outlet free. Do not press a desperate foe too hard."

If you permit no means of escape or settlement, the teacher warns, you ensure that your foe will fight to the death, exacting mass casualties on both sides. (Not a bad principle for managing family and workplace conflicts.)

Hence, in Sun Tzu's teaching, the shrewd general leaves his enemy an "outlet free." But here I may be too rosy. Giles clarifies that the Master may have intended this as a strategic ruse. Citing Chinese poet Tu Mu (803–852 A.D.), the sinologist observes:

> This does not mean that the enemy is to be allowed to escape. The object, as Tu Mu puts it, is "to make him believe that there is a road to safety, and thus prevent his fighting with the courage of despair." Tu Mu adds pleasantly: "After that, you may crush him."

If I had to put Sun Tzu's strategy into a nutshell, I would use one of his maxims: "Let your plans be dark and impenetrable as night, and when you move, fall like a thunderbolt."

In a sense, *The Art of War* is about *unlearning* the complexities of life and returning to the simple and true. Its unknown voice from millennia ago teaches us to strip away complication and thus attain highest effectiveness.

* * *

To honor the practicality of Sun Tzu's teaching, I end as I started: with the Master's principles.

Below are my twenty-three distillations of *The Art of War*'s insights. Where quotations appear, they are from Giles. Although I number these analects for convenience, none surpass the other.

1. "All warfare is based on deception." This is Sun Tzu's keynote; most tactics in his book rest on this principle.
2. Another of Sun Tzu's core principles is to *win without fighting.* Strength and foreknowledge ideally make combat unnecessary; victory is won by outmaneuvering or outflanking the enemy and thus breaking his nerve or resolve. A display of overwhelming might will also deter your adversary. There is a subtler dimension to this point: dominant nature—composed of the Way—along with knowledge and preparation foster irresistible advantage. *Tao Te Ching*: "The greatest conquerors are those who overcome their enemies without strife."
3. Sun Tzu had no respect for commanders who act from emotion or haste. Research, foreknowledge, deliberateness, and information-gathering—

including espionage—are central to his system and are, he argued, the surest means to victory. *Tao Te Ching*: "The best soldiers are not warlike; the best fighters do not lose their temper."

4. Although Sun Tzu warns against anger in a commander, he is not above using it as a tactical goad among troops or adversaries.
5. Sun Tzu cautioned against the drain of extended campaigns or drawn-out occupations. Compare to *Tao Te Ching*: "The good man wins a victory and then stops; he will not go on to acts of violence." Also: "Where troops have been quartered, brambles and thorns spring up. In the track of great armies there must follow lean years."
6. Sun Tzu emphasized ability to "live off the land"—no army or exploratory mission can possibly bring all of its supplies with it. Plus, supply lines may get disrupted. Prepare to supplement your supplies from territory you enter.
7. Natural law dictates that where two parties are involved, the outcome depends on the *actions of both*. Hence, conditions may rapidly change.
8. The great warrior does not chase glory. His victory is so natural that it is not even noticed. The commander who seeks glory is prone to risk, extended campaigns, and massive loss. *Tao Te Ching*: "Winning, he boasteth not; he will not triumph; he shows no arrogance.

He wins because he cannot choose [i.e., it is natural]; after his victory he will not be overbearing."

9. Do not credit yourself for ordinary means and methods; seek *impeccable means.* No one is rewarded for just doing his job.
10. Sun Tzu places little stock in inspiration, which ebbs and flows, but rather seeks "method and discipline," which are permanent.
11. Sun Tzu advises the warrior to be like water: quiet, unnoticed, humble, dwelling at the lowest depths—but when fighting, water rushes downhill in an irresistible torrent and bursts through the enemy's defenses at their weakest point.
12. Water, being silent and lowly, goes unseen as it absorbs information about the enemy and landscape. *Tao Te Ching*: "He who raises himself on tiptoe cannot stand firm; he who stretches his legs wide apart cannot walk."
13. *Flexibility* is central to Sun Tzu's philosophy. Combinations are limitless. A commander must never grow comfortable with any one tactic. Tactics may repeat—with caution: losses result from repetition of a tactic that formerly brought victory but is unsuited to a new challenge.
14. Once an attack is decided on, it must be carried out with decisiveness, dedication, and ferocity. Otherwise *it is better not to attack.*

15. The warrior must never over-rely on any one person or factor.
16. Always arrive first on the battlefield.
17. Compel your forces to depend on each other for life and they will fight fiercely and uniformly.
18. Leave your soldiers no way out and they will fight intensely. In the West this is sometimes called "burning the fleet." This also displays your determination to foes.
19. Focus troops on the goal not the means to the goal; means are the concern of commanders.
20. Know your environment: use the current of nature.
21. Consider gravely the consequences of war. Sun Tzu: "A kingdom that has once been destroyed can never come again into being; nor can the dead ever be brought back to life."
22. Spies are highly valuable, especially a former minister bringing vital information into your camp.
23. Before seeking strict consistency in Sun Tzu's statements, note the *Tao Te Ching*: "The truest sayings are paradoxical."

The Art of War is not for the high-conflict persona. It is for one who seeks to prevail when conflict is unavoidable. It goes well with a strong punch—which, as Master Sun teaches, may make battle unnecessary.

ELEVEN

"Be, and Not Seem"

Those of us in the culture of spiritual search often hear the terms *realized, enlightened, awakened*, and so forth. These superlatives are rarely defined even as they are commonly used.

I question the existence of a realized being, obviously willing to abide exception. Writing these words at age sixty, after many years in the search in both traditional and esoteric precincts, I have never met one. A friend leads a dojo and has spent significant time at Buddhist monasteries in Japan. "Have you," I once asked him, "ever once met a realized man?" His answer: "No."

Recent to this writing, a viewer wrote me on YouTube:

> On the subject of awakened and realized people, yes there are awakened and realized people but

> they are still human. They still experience anxiety and depression. Awakened people aren't free from suffering. They are awake to who they are and how the world really is. How will you know an awakened person? You will feel accepted and loved by them.

I find that a reasonable if satisfied definition. It is not my own.

My perception of a realized being derives from the teachings of G.I. Gurdjieff. A realized or awakened being possesses an "I." By which is meant a central *I* from which *to do*.

That is not the individual's situation. We are in pieces. Our thoughts, emotions, and physicality all run on their own tracks. Were that not so, there would be no addictions, outbursts of rage, harmful self-distractions, and so forth. The body wants something—food, sex, sleep, whatever—and the intellect has no more power to oppose it than a paddler does a mighty current, if such effort is even expended. The emotions, like a horse, kick in fear, and no degree of intellectualizing or inner talking can change that.

What I write is a confectionary description of man's real predicament, or what Gurdjieff called "The Terror-of-the-Situation": man pursues war, i.e., me and all of us; man must be right; man invokes high-sounding ethics while living from "I like" and "I don't like."

I believe that humanity's situation is near-impossible. Hence, I virtually never use terms to connote openings that are not there, at least evidently. What my YouTube correspondent describes is not, I believe, *awakening* but *suffering*—of a right sort.

I hear from some seekers that *their* teacher is enlightened. But three-dimensional normies cannot detect it. There is, to my ears, vanity in this. If one's teacher is enlightened that makes the student an apostle, hence the eagerness to school others.

This confusion is deepened by the conceit or unawareness of soi-disant teachers themselves. A friend of mine recently joined a panel of New Age spiritual bigwigs, some of whom are household names. During a shared moment backstage, he said to his co-panelists: "Wow, that audience is looking at us like we actually know something."

To a person, they stared blankly at him—and then argued, *"no, we know things."*

I am acquainted with some of these panelists. Some of them I have published, share colleagues, or collaborate with from time to time. Among them are people who struggle with rage—but never on stage. Some break their word—but never on stage. I once interviewed one for a now-defunct streaming talk show. In between what seemed like fifteen-minute answers, more recitations than responses, into which I could hardly interject a word, he went on and on about enlightenment and non-attachment and (spare me) sensing "the thinker behind the thoughts." I know this person professionally as someone who has flown into rage when his book did not hit the *New York Times* Bestseller List. Sounds like me.

And here is the point: we need greater transparency from spiritual eminences. Rather than dirge-like monologues about our "being afraid of how great we are" or the healing powers of forgiveness ("you forgive for yourself . . .") or one of a hundred fortune-cookie scrolls of wisdom, which we've all heard if rarely verified, *we must hear from the guru who has failed.*

I am not a teacher. I am seeker. If I can fulfill that role, it is enough. In my writing and talks I am self-disclosing not for some lurid attention-grab but because my life is unexceptional and what I have experienced, and where I have failed, may provide commonality from which to search.

Some who use the terms I critique eagerly share their own stories of breakthrough. But these are memories. If a moment cannot be summoned now, what is it but showing one's vacation photos? Wake that same person at an inconvenient hour, in an unfamiliar place, to perform an unpleasant task and you will see how enlightened we are.

I once separated from a remarkable teacher whose judgment I believe had slipped. We were out of touch for weeks. People assumed (and still do) that we had no contact. This was not so. He contacted me, not to ask me to return or to make peace, but rather he asked me to meet one-on-one with prospective newcomers to the group he led. His action, followed soon after by his death, was the closest thing I have witnessed to realized. Were he here, he would probably say, "Let's take me out of it."

The final gift he extended—one of vulnerability and trust—soon brought my concerns in this chapter into astringent light. Meeting with these earnest and thinking newcomers, something made me uneasy. They gazed hopefully at me across the table, maybe at a restaurant or coffee shop, as though I was "the man with the plan"—as if I possessed some special answers, insight, or gate key.

I had none.

My teacher asked me to meet with an orthodox Jew. "He'll want to know all about you," he said, probably referencing his curiosity over our shared background. I was uncomfortable with this. I did not reply. My teacher died soon after. It was our last contact. This saddens me. He would probably ask: "Why?" We are all filled with failures, automaticities, and emotions we do not understand.

No Inspiration

"Be, and not seem." Ralph Waldo Emerson wrote this in his 1841 "Spiritual Laws." I try. Facts expose me.

On Halloween 2025, a gifted friend said she was inspired by a video I had posted. I told her the truth. I am mildly paranoid, irritable, vain, prone to mood swings, and filled with stupidities and helplessness too private to share. I have hurt others through selfishness and self-fixation.

Having previously worked in publishing for twenty-seven years—most of that time in spiritual publishing—I have, to borrow a phrase, seen how the sausages get made. Your favorite inspirational, self-help, and spiritually aware authors are, by and large, figures of weakness, ego, passive aggression, and rage. They send people into bathrooms crying. I have sent people home crying. I am sickened by it and hope I never do so again.

I once interviewed one of the top-selling spiritual authors of the last century. Someone made famous by Oprah. It was for a small metaphysical magazine. The entire arrangement was one of comity, ease, and friendliness—or so I thought. "Is it okay if I tape our interview?" I asked perfunctorily. He agreed—but added balefully, "I am taping it myself." He was counter-taping our talk—out of suspicion. That is not an exception; it is a core sample. I have dozens, many far more dispiriting.

My point in this chapter is not "spilling the beans" on spiritual celebrities. It is asking, starting with a non-celebrity like me, that spiritual writers, thinkers, and seekers up their game in terms of public honesty. That they reveal their suffering, insecurity, aggression, and egotism. Anything less misleads the seeker. Worse, obfuscation propagates a self-serving mirage of a persona to which readers and listeners believe they can aspire. Such practice proffers a soft lie about the human situation.

It Is Not Possible

Work on self is more than elusive. It is often illusory due to false application of terms like realized, enlightened, or awakened in a spiritual culture that reflexively accepts concepts of personal evolution without understanding man's true state.

"The problem with New Age books," my teacher said, "is that they actually make the work seem possible."

An author I like once countered, "But, Mitch, it is possible." It is not. Not as we are: under conditions of mechanical existence and sleep.

The human situation is one of absolute automaticity. We make vows in chairs. We violate them at the slightest friction of life. Slender hope exists for man—but only in a different, finer state, where choice, destiny, and *doing* exist. I dislike even writing that because the words summon imagination of a state I do not know.

The only thing that any of us can sincerely hope to exercise is a question. It is the one indestructible facet of the search. You cannot lie and question simultaneously.

Maybe I am too harsh. The man-machine does not know he is lying. He perceives self as reasonable, if not noble. Contrary impressions cannot enter. Gurdjieff called this a "buffer."

A Lie

A mentor once lied to me. (He also lied about me, a different story.) During my publishing days, I arranged for a now-defunct spiritual journal to freely excerpt a chapter of his in exchange for a credit line to the book. The credit line did not appear. The journal's editor, a philosopher and poet, dodged my calls.

This arrangement, made on a handshake, was personally and professionally meaningful to me. It also saved the publication money and averted corporate bureaucracy. Further, the journal agreed to—then reneged on—a corrective. I could not understand its dereliction.

Looking back, I realize that there probably existed some kind of undisclosed financial arrangement, e.g., the author solicited money under the table after I provided the excerpt gratis, triggering this sketchy behavior. I had the clout to pull Penguin's ads. I did not use it.

Authors and speakers excel at theater. They—and I—also like attention. Hence, in public settings they appear poised, gracious, and accountable. That is a stage persona. Most do not even realize it. Picnics do not reveal the person. Including to him.

My self is not revealed at book signings. It is revealed when I delay preparing dinner because I cannot figure out a tech problem (a source of embarrassing anguish) or I am distractingly alarmed by an IRS letter or I freak out on a "customer service" call with health insurers. The latter being a criminal enterprise grants me a half-pass. Circumstances being what they are, we all receive half-passes.

A Secret

Earlier I noted the experience of newcomers gazing longingly at me. That is what each one of us does when first meeting a therapist, minister, spiritual teacher, channeler, or what have you.

Let me whisper a secret. *They revel in it.* They subtly—perhaps unknowingly—register the theatricality and treasure (if not abuse) their leading role.

Do not fall for it, as some half-teachers themselves do. Protect yourself. Seekers are not suppliants. Social, cultural, or spiritual authority is often accidental.

My teacher once gave me a book, *Monkey on a Stick: Murder, Madness, and the Hare Krishnas.* "Here, read this," he said. "You'll never want to belong to any spiritual organization again."

As it happens, he was, in the early 1970s, a member of the Hare Krishna order, which had its first New York City headquarters—still there—in a little storefront in the East Village on First Avenue near Houston Street.

The HK movement was still getting started and they hadn't a stick of furniture. But they did have the guidance of Swami Prabhupada (1896–1977) whom my teacher—a figure of real values and seriousness—considered a realized man. It was a term I never heard him otherwise use.

One day, Swami Prabhupada lent my friend a sacred Hindu book. Since there was no furniture in the place, he had nowhere to put it down. Not wanting to place it on the floor, he put it on top of his shoes by the door.

My friend did not yet realize that within traditional Hinduism shoes are considered filthy and profane. When the Swami saw what he had done, he grew angry and told my teacher, "I see that you do not know how to properly treat a scared book—return it to me at once!"

My friend told me: "I realized at that moment that this man could not be my teacher. Because he could not see me."

My friend would never disrespect a hallowed book. Never. That the Swami could not see that meant that my friend would have to leave and find a guide elsewhere. He soon grew dedicated to the Gurdjieff work, where I knew him.

Ironically—although I think purposefully—this cycle repeated in our lives. It may be intrinsic to the teacher-student relationship. My love for him has never once flagged.

In any case, the lesson I take from his story is this: you must never compromise your sense of self on the path. If a "realized" person (I have never met one) misjudges you, act on that knowledge. The path requires hardy travelers, not cowering rabbits.

The path also requires people with sufficient intellect not to have to show off how smart or in-the-know they are. Let someone else be smart. But never relinquish your being.

And beware of students who enforce the teacher's sanctity. They are often defending their own. When I posted this story on Substack, I received a proper English tongue-lashing from a Prabhupada acolyte who was certain his Swami was more perceptive than I knew and that my friend had failed a test. I can see his side of it. But nothing abrogates the judgment of the individual. If he or she is wrong, all the better that they move on.

The search, if genuine, must be exquisitely voluntary. "A real esoteric group," Jacob Needleman told me, "is very difficult to find and very easy to leave. A fake group is the exact opposite."

* * *

That said, I am by no means issuing a call for insouciance. If you cannot recognize a sensitive teacher or senior colleague, you will never know wisdom or at least knowledge. You will recite. And you will bask in the sound of it.

The pivot point of the spiritual search is capacity to recognize who you are talking to. In that vein, never mistake access for parity. Ability to exchange with a senior colleague or insightful person, and to do so freely, heightens the need to understand the privilege of contact.

How do you know authenticity? I alluded to it in the first chapter. The dividing line between artifice and verity is generosity. No one, student or scholar, is worthy without it. But remember: "Every stick has two ends." The Talmudic digest *Pirkei Avos* ("Ethics of the Fathers") warns:

> Warm yourself by the fire of the scholars, but beware of their glowing coals, lest you burn yourself; for the bite of scholars is as hurtful as that of a fox, their sting is as deadly as that of a scorpion, their hiss is like that of a serpent, and all their words are like coals of fire. (2:10, Hebrew Publishing Company, 1949)

I deplore explaining wisdom. Here I must. The master describes not a teacher's license but a student's unawareness. Teachers may, at times, instruct from confrontation. That has a place. Yet: I have, at times, witnessed confrontation overused, as a scalpel becomes a weapon. Or worse, used by those who have not earned it. I once issued a challenge in my heart to senior colleagues. I did not speak it aloud. It shifted energy: "I want to see you go twenty-four hours without having to insult someone to make a point."

A Mistake

My teacher once made a mistake. After excessive delay, I was granted entry to a movements class. My second son was just born and I was holding down a corporate publishing job while completing my first book. I sometimes had difficulty getting to class.

I did not like the class. I found the instructors affected in their sternness and witnessed some guy who played the piano, who I assume was considered a senior figure, scream—literally scream—at people who were foolishly talking in class one night. I disdained the mouse-like scurrying many students displayed. I was terrible at the movements. This was no deterrence to me.

"I just saved you from getting kicked out of your movements class," my teacher told me at lunch. I did not like that. Most of the students were childless, divorced, or single, sometimes at a holding-pattern in their jobs. Time was a different measure for them. Hence, the work became its own culture.

Greater effort could be expected of me—that is fair. But threats sat poorly with me. There exists a widely heard expression, *When the student is ready, the teacher appears.* It is traceable in principle to Theosophist Mabel Collins' 1885 *Light on the Path*: "For when the disciple is ready the Master is ready also." If true, the maxim must also be true in its opposite. For the first and only time I wondered, in reference to that class, if the teachers were ready. I do not wish to set too high a standard. But when discipline is used, discipline is the obligation of both parties.

A Call

I am not endorsing morbid self-revelation, which can become theater of its own. There are humiliating things I am not saying about myself. Rather, I am asking only that those of us communicating about spirituality in public spaces and on social media attempt greater transparency.

Some popular voices are incapable of self-exposure. Due to "brand"—may that word wither from the vernacular—or buffers or both, they actually believe they are developed if not realized people. Notwithstanding phone-yelling at editorial assistants (a favorite of "spiritual activists"), making idiosyncratic demands in restaurants (one bestselling spiritual author orders multiple meals to sample each), and sending rambling late-night emails. I have erased every one so that no record exists. If you want to send me an obnoxious email, feel free—I make a practice of deleting them to avoid self-justification of my own.

The issue is not one of flaws. Or of personality. Or of "being human." It is of fundamental repetition and mechanicality in being. Regardless of talent for speaking, writing, or voracious reading.

You know no one—no one—until you have witnessed that person under stress. This occurs outside the theater of temple, church, dojo, bookstore, streaming video, classroom, and event space.

Who among my spiritual heroes would I like to meet? I suppose Neville Goddard—there is much I would like to talk over with him. But I can live with or without it because I know that every last one of them, with the exception of Gurdjieff, was as helpless as I am in conditions of adversity. Neville died from drinking too much.

I drink and smoke weed nearly every night. Next time you feel inspired by me, keep that in mind. (As I write these words, such practices are loosening a bit—I credit Transcendental Meditation.)

Some will say that in this chapter I am too easy on myself. They are wrong. Because they do not know what I experience. Others will say the opposite. They, too, are wrong—for the same reason.

The wisest thing a mentor told me arrived after I apologized for an angry outburst. It may sound like a cliche. It is not—because it is sincere: "We are all in the same boat." Spiritual eminences owe it to readers and listeners to be frank about this. If they understand it. Any who do not have little or nothing to offer you.

Again, a question and a lie cannot coexist. We need a deepened question. To be, and not seem—even, or especially, in failure—points toward it.

TWELVE

Against Forgiveness

In quarters of the spiritual search, you will hear encouragement to verify things for yourself. That is often half-sincere. In practice, it generally means: when you have verified my point of view, return. Verification is not consensus. Use it authentically.

Verification has led me to question foundational customs, or familiarities, framed as bestowed truth, including the urge to forgive.

Forgiveness is not a toll entry to selfhood. You can forgive or not forgive.

"I don't do forgiveness," says the anti-heroine of the simultaneously verisimilitudinous and disappointing horror film *A Dark Song*.* I stand with her.

---

* See the postscript to this chapter for a fuller discussion of this significant movie.

I prefer abiding a wound and surpassing it to forgiving its perpetrator.

When I harm someone, through selfishness or neglect—I don't do spite—I apologize, without reservation or qualification.

Anything less ("I'm sorry but. . . ," or the grotesque, "I'm sorry if I offended you . . .") is not only a false apology—it is worse: perpetrating further harm on an injured person.

The sufferer owes me nothing. Even if he or she, like me, behaves wrongly that is a separate matter from my remorse. And I never—ever—ask forgiveness. It burdens the wounded. It takes a decision from that person. It is perniciously selfish.

* * *

During the first year of the COVID lockdown, the owner of an audiobook studio made it nearly impossible for me to earn a living. At that time, I was supporting myself and my household in large measure through audio narration. My publisher had a longstanding contract with this studio proprietor and we had contributed routinely and reliably to his bottom line.

He told the story that some germophobic client had booked hours of recording time; the depicted client insisted on a full cleaning and twenty-four hour wait period between recording sessions. Hence, I was shit out of luck.

When I finally returned to the studio, after my publisher's repeat intervention, I found it unclean with a used tissue on the mic lectern. Gross. No indicator of a fastidious client. I think the owner was using the lockdown as a cover story for shifting his business away from live recording to postproduction, which is more remunerative. Any business owner is free to shift his model—but ditching loyal clients during a lockdown? Making it impossible for me to work?

The proprietor emailed me a semi-apology. "Forgive me," he wrote, using those words. Not happening.

Remorse Is Mine to Carry

When you do wrong, if you cannot help it beforehand, stand up and say sorry. Then stop talking. If you feel remorse, all the better. G.I. Gurdjieff wrote in *Beelzebub's Tales to His Grandson* that we all have an "inner 'Evil-God', called 'Self-Calming'." Asking forgiveness is among the deceptions of Self-Calming.

Extending forgiveness is an entirely private matter. It is not a "spiritual law." It is not done "for yourself." It does not ensure corrected karma. It is not freedom from the injury suffered. All of those framings, whatever their vintage or provenance, are decisions made by another.

Early in my publishing days, we met with a rabbi—one of many—who wanted to write a book of popular theology. "First we have to forgive ourselves," he said (more than once). This was nearly thirty years ago. That proposition—along with other psycho-spiritual familiarities struck me then and now as a bromide.

I admire the Twelve Steps. I respect the critical role of forgiveness in Alcoholics Anonymous. But I do not see forgiveness as an always-must or evergreen. Treating it as such flattens human experience.

The seeking person has, I believe, been philosophically, therapeutically, and theologically oversold on forgiveness as requisite doctrine and inceptive step to recovery or releasing pathos. There exist other steps. Some of them—depending on persona and perspective—more effective and more right. I state this from experience and assume that no trait or insight is limited to any one life.

Forgiveness Is Not Shared Property

Nearly every religious tradition, as well as most new religious movements, affirms the necessity of forgiveness. Turning the other cheek and forgiving the transgressor form the heart of Christianity. This principle is less pronounced but still deeply seated in Judaism. Forgiveness resonates, albeit with different rationales, in Vedic traditions. To forgive is at the center of modern spiritual philosophies like *A Course in Miracles*.

Colleagues whom I respect have argued to me, with formidability, that without forgiveness history could not march forward. My friend Richard Smoley writes with sterling precision in his 2015 book *The Deal*, which I was proud to publish, that forgiveness is the sole escape hatch we are given from our karma—and that we will soon enough require the same forgiveness we offer another. (If you disagree with my perspective in this chapter, or even if you agree with it, read Richard's book—it is of immense value on the path.)

Forgiveness is a topic that—ironically—engenders polarized opinion. One morning in 2020, a piece of writing like this one came pouring out of me. It arose from asking myself: What if what we are told about the traditional imperative of forgiveness is not universally or even necessarily true? This question is not encouraged.

Editors and gatekeepers, to a person, rejected my article. (This also occurred with my 2020 counter-obituary of pseudo-skeptic James Randi.) Truth, when it arrives, is usually unpopular. Going it alone, I posted the piece on *Medium* as "Forgiveness: A Dissent."

To my surprise, it received a warm upswell of reader response. Many expressed elation that someone was willing to question how religionists, therapists, and peers often urge us to forgive, as though they have a stake in the matter. One wrote me:

> I am so relieved to read this argument. I find that forgiveness gets forced on us, and people get upset with me if I say I haven't forgiven, even if they have nothing to do with the situation themselves!

Abiding vs Forgiving

Before my dissenting position reached me in 2020, I worked intently with forgiveness for seven years. I prayed, pondered, assayed, and studied. I believe I have earned it when I question the ethical and spiritual centrality of forgiveness.

My reason, finally, is simple: I believe that the moral suasion to forgive often proves fitful in outcome and produces inner division that gets diverted into other, sometimes hostile or self-negating behaviors. That does not mean forgiveness is unwarranted in given situations. Nor that it has not healed wounds. It means only that I reject forgiveness as a blanket rule, religious imperative, or ethical necessity.

Am I arguing for revenge? Not necessarily. I do, however, like that in the serialized novel *Consuelo* (1842–

1843) by "George Sand," the byline of France's clandestine woman of letters Amantine Lucile Aurore Dupin de Francueil (1804–1876), Satan appears in the heroine's dream as "the archangel of legitimate resolution."

I contend that a finer, more realistic, and nobler principle than forgiveness appears in *abiding.* In enduring hurt, suffering, wounding, or trespass with the realism that life is reciprocal, suffering is inevitable—and the vow that another person's violation (the root of violence) is wind at your back for progress toward what you must be and do in life.

Are you defeated? Consider the words of Shakespeare's temporary victor Lady Macbeth: "'Tis safer to be that which we destroy / Than by destruction dwell in doubtful joy."

Redress Is Lawful

As I have widely documented, we as a human community have amassed evidence, not only from the testimony of seekers, but from studies in psychical research, relativity, retrocausality, quantum theory, and neuroplasticity, among others, to conclude that physicalism and linear time are conceptually insufficient to cover all the bases of life.

Thoughts impact neural pathways. Anomalous transfer of information, or ESP, is statistically settled. Time bends based on velocity and gravity. Time violates its perceived "straight arrow." Observation effectively determines quantum locality. Quantum computing surpasses the limits of known time and possibly the rules of unidimensional reality. We can debate terms, conditions, and consistency, but what I describe exists.

Hence, to speak of reciprocity is more than just metaphor. On rationalistic terms alone, the wheels of redress are no more stoppable than the cycles of planets. What I visit upon another person I ultimately, or in more immediate fashion, visit upon myself, due to our interconnected metaphysics.

Ah ha! I have just argued for forgiveness. Not exactly. The good you experience results from debt paid. Nothing in life can be given. All must be labored for, indirectly or not. Your wound is, even now, cauterizing into something new and potentially vital. It is a natural law. This chapter could not have been written without this verity. You can, I warrant, summon similar ones in your existence.

I do not know why, but the generation before me used to pilfer packets of the artificial sweetener *Sweet'n Low* from diners. Maybe it was not widely available in grocery stores. Grabbing a few packets one day, my teacher told me: "I'll pay for my existence but, goddamn it, I won't pay for *Sweet'n Low.*" His joke, like all jokes, concealed truth: life is payment. You can see forgiveness as payment. But consider: in suffering, you have already paid.

The best argument for forgiveness is that I have hurt people unaware. This is undoubtedly true. Hence, to forgive another is, on my terms, payment for hurt unwarranted and unknown. Yet—currency and exchange are mysterious processes, a point to which I now turn.

"Real Feeling Is Impersonal"

I generally eschew the term karma. In Vedic teaching, karma is conceptually so vast and objective that it is difficult—or worse still, easy—to reference it in isolation.

For one thing, opposing ends of karma are so immense that we are rarely granted to perceive its workings. Karma can be near-impossible to negotiate or envisage.

In that vein, I offer a response by Lord John Pentland, one of Gurdjieff's principal students, from a group meeting transcribed in the 1997 book *Exchanges Within*. Lord Pentland does not use the term karma here and I hope I do not err in projecting that onto his statement. But I consider my framing accurate.

Real feeling is impersonal. It comes from very high in the scale and it connects everything together. The story which I've several times used the last couple of weeks to illustrate that is the story of Brahma. He's supposed to be absolute god in India, and he was taking a nap one day when a very high Brahman—it comes from Brahma, Brahman, it's the highest caste—came with a little child, his son that had died, and said, "Look, Lord Brahma, the first-born son has died. There's something gone wrong down on the earth. You shouldn't have allowed that. Would you look into it?" So Brahma had to get up and dress and so forth and went down to earth and discovered that there was this temple. And a Sudra—that means the lowest caste, untouchable caste—had been affected by some very deep wish and had found his way into the temple. Appalling thing to happen. So Brahma took one look at the Sudra and he immediately died. One look at Brahma was enough to kill the Sudra. However, this had the effect of fulfilling the Sudra's wish because he died in the temple. So he was saved. At the same time, the little infant immediately was again breathing. You understand?

Well, that is an impersonal story, if you like. Yes? But that's rather strong meat for some of us.

> That's why I say, although there's relativity, you would have to a little bit expand your horizon to try and get the twin ends of the scale. Yes?

I believe Nietzsche reflected some understanding of this when he wrote in *Beyond Good and Evil* in 1886: "One *has* to repay good and ill—but why precisely to the person who has done us good or ill?" (From Walter Kaufmann's 1966 translation.)

I consider everything part of a scale. Sometimes we can detect one portion of the scale or arc of existence. The scale of karma that we are granted to understand could perhaps be described as reciprocity. Reciprocity, in terms of consequence, means doing nothing to disrupt another's capacity to search. If I have a core ethic on the path, that is it. Refusing to circumvent another's search also means neither condescending to nor denigrating another. Those who need this statement are, as a rule, those who think they do not. That, too, is payment.

"Opposition is True Friendship"

I believe that a better—by which I mean realer—response to pain is using it as a goad to development. Authentic positive thinking means evaluating circumstances based on their capacity for self-development.

William Blake (1757–1827) wrote in *The Marriage of Heaven and Hell*: "Opposition is true Friendship." Live with that for six months.

Opposition not only exposes where I need fortification but spurs creative powers of necessity. Without friction we would remain intellectual and emotional children. I see this as the esoteric meaning behind the expulsion from the Garden: the snake emancipated. With emancipation came suffering. And so the individual became creative actor versus object.

Should Adam and Eve forgive Yahweh for the inconceivable cruelty of condemning humanity to forever being born in sin for ancestral violation? Does the parabolic sacrifice of his son redeem or compound that sentence? Friction is neither to be forgiven nor understood (especially when ersatz understanding results in ethical paralysis). Friction is our human and spiritual situation.

Looking back at my six decades of life, most harm I have suffered has been in the name of helping me. Someone recently messaged: "Hello Mitch, I enjoyed watching some of your lectures. I just want to say: infinite love will overcome evil." I replied: "Since some people consider my ideas 'evil' I am careful with statements about overcoming."

"No Law Can Be Sacred"

In his 1841 "Self-Reliance," Ralph Waldo Emerson cast all this in a refreshing light. Cultural affinity and the need for brand-media and academic copy are conscripting Emerson to critical mockery.

The New York Times Magazine

RIFF

The Foul Reign of Emerson's 'Self-Reliance'

Share full article

Tom Gauld

By Benjamin Anastas
Dec. 2, 2011

My first exposure to the high-flown pap of Ralph Waldo Emerson's "Self-Reliance" came in a basement classroom at the private boys'

I often disparage mainstream letters. There is, I must admit, envy in this. (Some of it class-based.) Earlier in my career, I labored, with some success, to attain mainstream bylines as a means of validation. That effort was arduous and, I believe, necessary. But having sniffed the glove of that world (as well as academic publishing), I reject it. Its intellectual parameters are dispiritingly narrow. Materialism is a given. Doubt without rigor is rewarded. There is no antidote for that. But such trends indicate why seekers must eschew commentary for source material.

Here is Emerson's passage:

> I remember an answer which when quite young I was prompted to make to a valued adviser, who was wont to importune me with the dear old doctrines of the church. On my saying, What have I to do with the sacredness of traditions, if I live wholly from within? my friend suggested,—"But these impulses may be from below, not from above." I replied, "They do not seem to me to be such; but if I am the Devil's child, I will live then from the Devil." No law can be sacred to me but that of my nature.

A law, in order to be a law, must be ever-operative and binding. In that sense, I do not see forgiveness as an ethical or spiritual law. You are an intellectual, emotional, and physical being. Your perspective on and emergence from pain are intimate matters. The capacity to search implies this. Whatever you find, I ask only: let it come from your own nature.

Postscript: *A Dark Song*

In my opening, I venture mixed reference to the stirring 2016 horror film, *A Dark Song*. As the spouse of a feature filmmaker and the writer-producer-host of films myself, I venerate the arduous effort behind any feature. Hence, I wish to clarify and deepen my assessment of this significant movie, which divided opinion among occultists. To do so, I reproduce a segment from a 2022 interview with the 'zine *Brain Bleed*. My comments complement the argument in this chapter.

> **Brain Bleed**: I recently watched a film called *A Dark Song* by Liam Gavin on Shudder. I thought it was fantastic and when I was reading some commentary on it, people were saying that it was one of the most accurate depictions of occult practices they had seen on film. First of all, have you seen it and is that true? Second, whether you've seen it or not, what are your feelings on how the occult is presented and portrayed, particularly in horror films? Is it blasphemous and offensive to you, fair and accurate, or ridiculous but all in good fun?
>
> **Mitch**: I stumbled upon that film and had a similarly strong reaction to it. I found the figure of the

occultist incredibly well represented in demeanor, intellect, and character. In fact, he reminded me of my friend Richard Smoley, which is considerable praise. I found the rigor of the ceremonial rituals extremely well done, although that has fed division, particularly involving the use of Chinese calligraphy. I say the following not as a criticism, because I think it truly is an outstanding film, but rather as a comment on our thought habits as a culture. I am going to give away the ending—so beware. I felt that the appearance of the archangel at the end and the conversion of the heroine reflected a rote and almost commonplace capitulation to Abrahamic religious assumptions.

Think of it: when a religious paradigm is continually repeated, in any culture, its very familiarity assumes contours of foundational truth. But it's just a dominant thought system. Nothing more. When the film's heroine says, "I don't do forgiveness," I thought—well, bravo; here is someone who knows what she believes, who has a point of view, who has a purpose. Why does that need to be stripped away from her? Is it because good is "up there" and evil is "down there"—in the basement, literally and metaphysically, in this case?

The denouement seemed to me to finally submit this eerie, brilliantly crafted occult adventure to the metaphysics of a Sunday school class. Again, this is not so much a criticism of the film—which is ingenious on many levels—but a statement on the limits of our search and the nature of intellectual or spiritual habit.

THIRTEEN

What Is Evil?

I promised a hammer. We are entering a portion of *Esoterika* that might be seen as its weighted edge. I disdain performative heterodoxy. My work is that of a seeker. It is the product of search and rigor—often repeated on itself.

In the principle of reopening inherited premises, I use the following chapters to review core sources of religion and ethics, to the extent they have reached us, and sometimes find arteries of thought, and testing grounds of self, unfamiliar yet vital.

Such is the case with *evil.* A big word. Used too often. (Like love.) What is it?

We all have pet definitions. Usually, not always, they hinge on what I fear. Or what I absolve in self and blame in another.

G.I. Gurdjieff observed that the totality of man's lived philosophy is "I like" and "I do not like," "I want" and "I do not want." I see no reason to challenge that.

In the Talmudic digest *Pirkei Avos* ("Ethics of the Fathers"), a master tells his students: "Go and see which is the worst quality a man should shun."

One of them, Rabbi Simeon, replies: "One who borrows and does not repay. It is the same whether one borrows from man or from God."

Another disciple, Rabbi Elazar says, "An evil heart," meaning greed and spite. The master, Rabban Yohanan ben Zakkai, pronounces those the best words, "for in his words yours are included."

Amalgamizing these principles, another disciple, Rabbi Yosé, later comments: "Let your friend's property be as precious to you as your own."

Life Is Debt

What does it mean to borrow and not repay? This question prompts the colloquialism *Talmudic*: the point can be argued so serpentinely that its meaning grows obfuscated. Or, in the hands of a real student, deepened.

To avoid obscuration or over literalism, I offer a single dimension—and, I think, the chief dimension, the space between two points—of what it means to borrow and not repay.

Life is debt. Unseen, unknowable, and multitudinous causes underlie my existence. I have not earned them. No one reading these words is free from that principle.

On a quotidian scale, the very device on which these words are being received, whether physical book, phone, desktop, or some other, was produced through human suffering: workers unevenly paid, irreplaceable minerals harvested from Earth, disposable batteries fated to poison someone's soil, and so on. Think of how infinitesimal a fragment of debt is referenced.

Debt occurs transactionally, too—my greater concern here for its immediacy. I recently green-lit publication of a book that I thought was in public domain. I fancy myself a copyright expert. For the first time in my career, I was wrong. In Neil Gaiman's *Whatever Happened to the Caped Crusader?*, Batman's death is depicted in a multiverse. In one panel, the Dark Knight muses: "Sometimes I fall in battle. Sometimes I die hugely, bravely, saving the city . . . Sometimes it's a small, ironic, unnoticed death—I die rescuing a child from a fire or tackling a frightened pickpocket."

I will pay back every dollar of damage for my oversight.

We must pay for our existence, including damage we cause.

Don't Blame Me

I detest those who shirk their debts—or, worse still, ascribe them to others. I used to laugh in my publishing days as an acquiring editor. Whenever someone did not deliver his or her book (or heaven forbid return the money), it was, inevitably and always, my fault.

Of all the people whose books I contracted and who did not finish them, exactly one took responsibility and repaid the money. That was Tucker Carlson. There is no politics in my comment. But mark it in context of this chapter.

And what of the term borrowing? Aren't we all doing that? From every fragment of coal to every nuclear explosion, we are using the source of the sun. This has formed the basis of religious devotions across time. Esoterically, that is a manner of recognizing debt.

Why Are You Alive?

I realize that even my narrow framing of this principle can branch off in endless directions. "What about a nation's debt? . . . What about . . . ?" I will say that our debt as a species warrants consideration. If you knew how many animals suffered and died for your uplifting, you would make a whole new measure of your life. Writing of laboratory uses of animals, philosopher William James (1842–1910) in 1875 noted somberly of a vivisected dog: "his sufferings are having their effect—truth, and perhaps future human ease are being bought by them."

Properly felt, this history should drive me to my knees. That is debt.

Likewise the suffering of ancestors whose journey to this place—and the people that earlier migrants displaced—put me in debt. Others have perished, directly or indirectly, so that I exist. That is debt.

A small means of payment is desisting from complaint, especially within.

Piety Is Not Payment

I hesitate, however, to wax too broadly in this matter. Overreach is avoidance. People who bang the loudest drums about global justice (or religious goodness) are, as a rule, the least likely to help you move, smile at a child, water a houseplant, or rescue you from real trouble.

They judge, they do not love, if there is such a thing. I have never experienced a modicum of love, joy, or uplift from grim keepers of tabs over who occupies the "right side of history."

In the same James essay, which is unsigned from *The Nation*, he notes the valiant New Englanders who stifle research over concern for animal rights yet benefit from "a community which boils millions of lobsters alive every year to add a charm to its suppers." I am borrowing when I write this passage, which appears fundamentally (with different emphasis) in Russell B.

Goodman's "Thinking About Animals" in the 2016 *Nordic Wittgenstein Review*. That, too, is debt.

Honor Priorities

Part of debt means giving things their due at the proper time and place. "If you don't give something its right attention now," Jacob Needleman told me, "it will take all of your attention later."

This principle has endless applications but it must include raising of children and caring for loved ones. The night I began this chapter, I delayed dinner for a recovering person. My excuse was the artist's need to capture lightning in a jar. The consequence was petty neglect. Perhaps the two intermittently coexist.

But my debt cannot be cleansed: "creativity" is, in its way, selfish. In light of the principle I have cited—"one who borrows and does not repay"—evil is not a matter of religion, professed fealties, or social side-taking. It is conduct. All else is a dodge. Convenience is, in a banal sense, evil—especially when used to define evil.

That Day

Years back, *The New York Times* published my critique of an academic who foolishly structured a study on restaurant responses to food-borne illness by writing letters to eateries falsely claiming illness. The result was near-panic among restaurateurs, all of whom expressed urgent concern. Only a social scientist who has never engaged in commerce could fail to foresee this.

The Times published my letter on September 11, 2001. I confessed with shame to my teacher that I actually felt rueful over my letter running that day—it

The New York Times

Opinion

The Nightmare Meal That Wasn't

By

Sept. 11, 2001

To the Editor:

Re "Scholar Sets Off Gastronomic False Alarm" (front page, Sept. 8):

It may be easy to criticize the personal judgment shown by Frank Flynn, a Columbia Business School professor who sent a fictitious letter alleging food poisoning to 240 restaurants as part of a study to determine how they responded to complaints. But his error may suggest a broader problem within segments of academia.

Have we really come to the point where a professor at one of the country's top business schools is so apparently ignorant of the daily workings of businesses that he would believe that his letter of complaint would cause anything less than the upheaval that ensued?

Mr. Flynn's case contributes to an uncomfortable suspicion that a number of today's leading academicians lack what is called real-world experience.

MITCH HOROWITZ

New York, Sept. 10, 2001

would go unnoticed. "Why?" he asked, challenging my shame. People are selfish and petty. We grab. I like. My stupidity is not evil. It is ordinary.

I collected donations that day at a Red Cross table. I grow emotional as I write these words. A young boy, perhaps age five, approached the table and handed me an envelope filled with nickels. He had broken open his piggybank. If there is any hope for humanity, which I doubt, it is that boy.

"No one," Needleman told me, "could have taught him to do that."

The boy understood debt. G.I. Gurdjieff called this a "magnetic center." Those born with a magnetic center possess a question. I deem this a state of fineness, often in the emotions but also in the intellect, where a question can survive. A political activist once told me that such references "sound like eugenics." I said I would consider his statement. I did. I deem it the idiocy of categories—of sorting what we consider good and evil into familiarities.

In any case, I cannot repeat the boy's story in public. I will cry. I do not know why. And I am not interested in reading why on social media or in comment sections. It is the nature of truth.

Another person approached me that day at the table. An older middle-aged woman. She said she had lost her home in the explosion. *She's lying*, I thought. She was too monotone, not in the manner of someone in shock but rather of someone tentatively testing a statement or claim. A Red Cross worker factually confirmed my instinct. The woman, whatever her motive (I hardly care), wanted attention. On a day of suffering, she sought to take. It was a shade of difference from my selfishness—but a shade too far. I do not judge her. I measure.

My Bicycle Ticket

Several days before starting this chapter, I got ticketed in a sting operation when I pedaled my bike through a red-light intersection in Midtown Manhattan. I soon discovered that I could not pay my summons online but had to appear on a weekday morning at criminal court in Midtown (I live in Brooklyn).

This kind of court appearance is intended as a punitive measure, which falls disproportionally on wage-earning people and parents (or both) who must seek coverage for work or caregiving. I speak less for myself than for the bicycle delivery man whose living is earned almost solely through tips.

As I biked to court, I recalled the cop who ticketed me explaining that a lot of elderly people live in the neighborhood where I was pinched. Police were trying to reduce risks. A fair point. Still, I was not a happy camper.

I planned to plead guilty and tell the judge something about my general practice of bike safety, which is true. Maybe I would catch a break. But something interrupted my plans. As I docked my electric bike in Midtown on a chilly morning, I glanced over my shoulder and began walking across the bike lane onto the sidewalk. Like lightning, another cyclist (either on an ebike or racing bike) was on top of me. He yelled out in alarm and we collided—just. There were no injuries. "Yo, a little slower in Midtown, please," I said. He did not turn around. Probably wise.

My excuses were done. I signed into the court roster and was directed to wait outside the building. A man stood among us complaining loudly to any who would listen about how city government was doing this just to suck up money. He reminded me of nearly everyone I grew up with. An officer came out and

CRIMINAL COURT OF THE CITY OF NEW YORK
COUNTY OF NEW YORK
1 CENTRE STREET
NEW YORK, NY 10007

Oct 28, 2025 SUMMONS # 4459263332

RE: HOROWITZ, MITCHELL

As of the above referenced date, the NYPD has failed to file a legally acceptable accusatory instrument with this court. There is no need for you to return to court on the summons number referenced above.

RETAIN THIS NOTICE FOR YOUR RECORDS

sent me home: it turns out, the police had not filed the complaint.

I draw no hokey karmic linkage between events. I note only: we always believe we are right. Chance suggests that is fifty-percent correct. Before calling out someone as "evil," gaze into the cracked mirror. In general, the person looking back has as much debt as the accused.

Evil then is not some maleficent, ultimate polarity. That description serves vanity. Evil is the shirking of what sustains my life.

Postscript: On Quoting Talmud

Due to the nature of our *I-heard-it-somewhere* culture, quoting Talmud, as I sometimes do in my writing on esoteric and occult topics, is a fraught exercise. Misunderstandings abound. Social media has developed a subculture of skewed excerpts.

It is important to note that the Talmud—in addition to its myriad and sprawling tracts and varying traditions—was constructed in late antiquity as a literary tabernacle for an exiled nation. Hence, some tracts reflect the same civic judicialism as any law-based work of the Hebrew Bible (i.e., Old Testament).

Given the setting and nature of these late-antique and debate-prone texts, they are—literally—not understandable or accurate in excerpt form. Context is everything.

Among the reasons the term "Talmudic" entered our vernacular is because it connotes highly complex, tortuous parsing of a passage. This is what is required—and what the sages and students themselves felt was required. There exists no "literalist" meaning that easily discloses itself.

In that vein, observers sometimes post passages that—in isolation or absent commentary—appear pernicious. This perpetuates misunderstanding. A frequent example is Ketubot 11b.* The tract's intent is protecting the abused from being ineligible for marriage—not defending the perpetrator.

If you wish to experience the ethical Talmud—i.e., the true meaning at its heart—read the short, immensely powerful volume *Pirkei Avot* or "Ethics of the Fathers."

The phoneticism *avot* ("fathers") is also rendered *avos*. Both are the same. The pronunciation *avot* is Sephardic, i.e., Middle Eastern-North African-Persian, while *avos* is Ashkenazi, i.e., European. Even titles contain folds.

Ethics rescued me in adolescence (along with the Dead Kennedys). There exist myriad translations of *Ethics*, with one linked below.**

---

* https://sefaria.org/Ketubot.11a.14?lang=bi
** https://www.sefaria.org/Pirkei_Avot?tab=contents

I will share a parable (with my own emphasis) from *Pirkei Avot* 2:6: A student is walking in a cave and sees a skull floating in the dank waters. "How did you get here?" the student asks. "I used my words to drown others," the skull replies, "and they returned to drown me."

FOURTEEN

Anti-Serenity

This chapter and the next reveal a great deal about my current search. They are based in transparency. If I have taught my sons one thing, I hope it is to tell the truth. I detest absence of plain dealing in our relationships and culture, a point I am sure you have gleaned. Violation of truth is violation of another. More people are hurt by the common lies of daily existence, which include failure to keep one's word, than by all the acts of supposed evil we thunder over (on social media, of course).

One's philosophy is conduct. There is no other measure. We preen to philosophies, religions, and claims never acted upon. We stand revealed by whether we help a friend with money—or think, *really think*, before asking someone a diminishing question or making a statement that calls his or her worth into doubt. Hostility is often covert. It is, in that sense, cowardly. It runs riot. Do not be a source of it, whenever possible.

I have no treacly statements for you about love, which I cannot define. Generosity, which I can define, is a sounder measure than claims of love. Love without generosity is, once more, like feeding someone by reciting a recipe. My code: Develop yourself. Step carefully. Demonstrate truth-telling, honor, and solidarity for the wounded. Be generous with the few people you care for. If you are in a lifeboat—row. And never stop trying because it is all we have.

This chapter—and this book as a whole—may be, in effect (and without intention), a manifesto of the Lefthand Path, i.e., the path of power and attainment, rooted in tantric siddhis in the East and Promethean will in the West.

I like an 1872 painting "Prometheus Brings Fire" (opposite), by Heinrich Friedrich Füger (1751–1818). If you look at the hero's face, you see uncertainty. That is the expression of truth. Füger completed it one year before his death.

* * *

I neither condemn nor elevate suffering. To generalize about a suffering person is to render him or her one-dimensional.

Having lived in New York City nearly all my life, I encounter suffering that is sometimes confrontational. Recent to this writing, something of value was said

during such a confrontation. It was with someone who wanted money and who I had inadvertently pissed off. She got up in my space and said something I liked:

"Change what you cannot accept."

"I dig that," I said.

She thought (wrongly) that I was making fun of her. "You dig that? Do you know what that is?"

"Yes, it's the Serenity Prayer . . ."

"It's the Serenity Prayer in reverse," she said. "Do you know the Serenity Prayer?" I assured her I did. And I liked her iteration. It is at the back of my search.

* * *

Most Western spirituality stems from Abrahamic traditions—Judaism-Christianity-Islam—along with variations of Vedic, Taoist, shamanic, or Buddhist teachings. At a turning point in my search around 2018, I found these expressions, in both traditional and esoteric iterations, unsatisfying.

I sought a more self-driven path. One of attainment, proteanism, and self-expression.

Although I did not embark on my search with this intention—nor with foreordained resistance—I found that my approach coalesced with an outlook previously mentioned. It is sometimes called the Lefthand Path.

In classical terms, Lefthand practice is rooted in Tantric Vedism and roughly comparable to heterodox traditions such as Sufism in Islam and Kabbalah in Judaism, which themselves have many variants. "The name of the left-hand path," surmises historian Dave Evans in his 2007 *The History of British Magic After Crowley*, "seems to derive from this practice being linked to the left-hand side of the face of Shiva, the Hindu god of destruction."

I cannot venture a direct connection, but in another ancient parallel, the Hebrew spelling of Samael, archangel of death (sometimes conflated with Satan), סמאל, differs by one /s/ phoneme, *samech* (ס), from the term for left, שְׂמֹאל, which begins with *shin* (שׂ). Shin can mean creator or destroyer.

In modern parlance, the Lefthand Path is an ethical and spiritual outlook that could be described as "My Will Be Done." This concept is, I believe, a more honest philosophical antonym to the Scriptural invocation "Thy Will Be Done," which is often invoked with the same meaning covertly or, just as often, unconsciously.

We wish to attain—broadly defined—and hope that our strivings comport with those of a Higher Power, or what I call a Greater Force, featured here in a variant of the 1789 *Grand Etteilla Tarot*, sometimes *Le Jeu de Toth* ("The Game of Thoth") or *Livre de Thot*

("Book of Thoth")—the first deck expressly designed for divination.

In its spiritual sense, *lefthand* is rooted in the Vedic Sanskrit *vamachara* ("lefthanded attainment"). Its Western adoption, along with the often-associated reverse pentagram, originated, as with much else, in the work of occult explorer Madame H.P. Blavatsky (1831–1891). Volume I of her 1888 *The Secret Doctrine* depicts a "horns up" pentagram—among the first times the symbol resounded in the West. It also appears in earlier works such as Eliphas Lévi's 1855 *Ritual of High Magic* and Franz Hartmann's 1886 *Magic: Black and White.*

Blavatsky wrote: "The esoteric symbol of Kali Yuga is the five-pointed star reversed . . . the sign of human sorcery, with its two points (horns) turned heavenward, a position every Occultist will recognise as one of the 'left-hand,' and used in ceremonial magic."

Contemporary Christian scholar John Smulo—who has been called a "Left-Hand Christian philosopher"—agrees with this historical entry point but intriguingly adds: "another possible origin of the term could be found in Matthew's Gospel, where Jesus speaks of placing the sheep (followers of Christ) at his right hand, and the goats (those who didn't follow Christ) at his left hand (Matthew 25:33)." [1]

There likewise exist longstanding folk associations, as noted by Evans:

> However useful it would be to have maintained this moral equivalence, history intervenes here, with the left-hand side having long been ascribed to the negative, with dexterous being a right-handed term and sinistrous, hence literally sinister, being left-handed. A minority of people are left-handed, perhaps less than 10%, although the right-handed hegemony is something that was taught, often forcibly, in British schools in the earlier 20th Century.

Some contemporary seekers who identify with the Lefthand Path believe neither in deity nor extra-physicality but use ritual and symbol for the focus of will. This practice of radical selfhood can be highly integral, such as when working to overcome a limitation or achieve a hallowed form of self-expression. Lefthand practices are not necessarily about "getting stuff," although I defend that approach since an individual's private needs, whatever their nature, may be essential and substantive. Those who walk the Lefthand Path are often critical of mainstream religionists and "white magic" New Agers who, they say (with validity, I believe), often use obfuscatory or "sacred" language to pursue perfumed self-interest.

A Zen prison minister (now dead) offered a story I value. He was visiting some inmates and one approached him: "I've read all your books and I can't believe I'm meeting you!" The minister replied, "It's not the man but the message." Later, he felt remorse. This inmate had a moment of joy—yet he erased it for some pious "lesson."

In spiritual culture, I distrust overuse of terms like "ego," "non-attachment," and "non-identification." They are concepts that limit our outlook to decisions made, and for centuries repeated, within Western and Eastern religious frameworks. Such decisions may not be your own.

Relatedly, I am uneasy around religionists who avow dedication to "service." Personally, and after many years on the path, I have never encountered someone claiming the mantle of service who was not concealing a shiv behind his or her back. I write that as plainly as I have experienced it. In short, every spiritual principle (and the company espousing it) requires scrutiny by seekers in every generation.

All religions, whatever universal truths they offer, arise from and respond to particular cultural circumstances. Cultural circumstances facing most ancient believers involved almost certainly dying within the same caste they were born into. The invisible world was a leveler and means of justice. I reject that perspective: of temporal life as illusory and the ineffable as absolute truth. I consider life, seen or unseen, one whole, united by the principle that invests existence with purpose: *self-expression*.

The Lefthand Path is often conflated with the "dark side" or Satanism, although these comparisons are usually proffered with too little subtlety and understanding to prove meaningful. While the Lefthand Path is not necessarily Satanic, it by no means precludes exploration of Satanism on a seeker's own terms.

The concepts of Satan—rooted in the Hebrew השטן (*ha-sa-taan*), literally "The Satan" or the adversary (sometimes the prosecutor), or the Latin-derived Lucifer—*helel ben sahar* or הֵילֵל בֶּן־שָׁחַר (shining one, son of dawn), which originated in Isaiah 14:12 as a condemning metaphor of the Babylonian throne as falling star—are, I realize, cultural landmines.

While the term Satanism, depending on your perspective, summons images of maleficent darkness, absurdly fictitious abuse scandals [2], anti-conformist libertinism, or any number of other associations, there is, I believe, an authentic, if diffuse, esoteric tradition of Satanism in the West, from antiquity to modernity, encompassing intellectual, ethical, literary, and spiritual dimensions.

In addition to re-soundings of ancient themes, I find the esoteric tradition of Satanism enduring in the work of Romantic poets and writers, such as William Blake, Percy Bysshe Shelley (1792–1822), and Lord Byron (1788–1824), who posited the Satanic as a force of rebellion, usurpation, overturning of staid or calcified structures, persistent questioning, rejection of conformity, and refusal of hive mentality. This is my perspective.

An antecedent for this outlook of radical selfhood appears in John Milton's (1608–1674) 1667 *Paradise Lost*, where Satan famously declares: "Here we may reign secure, and in my choice / To reign is worth ambition though in Hell: / Better to reign in Hell, then serve in Heav'n." In actuality, the precursor to Milton's lines may come from the mouth of Julius Caesar (100–44 B.C.), at least as posthumously recorded by ancient historian Plutarch (c. 46–119 A.D.):

> We are told that, as he was crossing the Alps and passing by a barbarian village which had very few inhabitants and was a sorry sight, his companions asked with mirth and laughter, "Can it be that here too there are ambitious strifes for office, struggles for primacy, and mutual jealousies of powerful men?" Whereupon Caesar said to them in all seriousness, "I would rather be first here than second at Rome." [3]

Yet I also distrust a go-it-alone approach to life. I believe in cosmic reciprocity, or what is sometimes, albeit in a flattened-out form, called karma. (On this count, refer to the consideration of karma in chapter twelve.) My spiritual, by which I mean extraphysical, outlook abides a core of human commonality, something reinforced by my interest in psychical research. Hence, my search is nonviolent. That does not mean abstaining from self-defense but rather doing nothing to knowingly deny another the same reach for human potential that I reserve for myself. In that regard, I do not seek to love my neighbor. But I do seek to leave him alone; except if solidaristically called to his defense.

For similar reasons, as seen, I challenge the imperative of forgiveness. I believe that the moral suasion to forgive often places the individual in an unnatural position and produces inner division that gets diverted into other, often hostile or self-negating behaviors. That does not mean forgiveness is unwarranted in given situations. Nor that it has not healed wounds. It means only that I reject forgiveness as a blanket rule, spiritual requirement, or ethical necessity. I find a more natural and realistic ethic in abiding: using injustice as a goad to something greater.

New Thought mystic Neville Goddard observed in a lecture of March 17, 1972, the year of his death, that a drama teacher once cruelly debased him. The British-

Barbadian youth, who had traveled alone to New York City at age seventeen to study theater, spoke in an Anglo-Caribbean accent, which his instructor deemed a career-killer:

> My own disappointments in my world led up to whatever I am doing today. When the teacher in my school, I could ill afford the $500 that my father gave me to go to this small school in New York City, and she made me the goat. She called me out before an audience of about forty students. And she said, "Now listen to him speak. He will never earn a living using his voice."
>
> She should not have done that, but she did it—but she didn't know the kind of person that she was talking about. Instead of going down into the grave and burying my head in shame, I was determined that I would actually disprove her.
>
> It did something to me when she said to me, "you will never earn"—to the class, using me as the guinea pig to show them what not to do—and so, she said, I spoke with a guttural voice and I spoke with this very heavy accent, and I will never use my voice to earn a living . . .
>
> We all went to this school and this teacher simply singled me out to make some little, well, exhibition of what I should not be doing in class. But I

> went home and I was so annoyed that I had lost my father's $500 or $600 that he gave me for the six-months course, but I was determined that she was false, that she was wrong.
>
> So, I went to the end. I went to the end and actually felt that I was facing an audience and unembarrassed that I could talk and talk and talk forever without notes, no notes.

When I first wrote about Neville in 2005 for *Science of Mind* magazine he was a near unknown even within many New Thought circles. My boss, himself a New Thought minister, needled me that I was only interested in the teacher due to his obscurity and that my article might find commensurate readership. I used his comments in the same way that Neville used his drama teacher's. As it happened, the article ignited a *Nevillelution.* Neville is today one of the most highly regarded spiritual orators of the twentieth century—and among the most widely read metaphysical voices of our own. His vast range of recorded lectures amass hits in the millions online.

The mystic taught a radical system of thought causation in which your imagination is God. He used expressly Christian terms and points of reference, even if dramatically redefined. This has led some seekers to ask how I can consider myself a student of Neville's thought.

I maintain correspondence with incarcerates. One who was freed recent to this writing wrote me in April 2022 the following passage. Although it is not necessarily how I would put things myself, I found her observation keen. An outsider may see my work better than I do. It is quoted with the writer's permission:

> . . . you really aren't deviating from the teachings of Neville Goddard, and I find it amusing that people miss that. He, as you know, taught about Christ consciousness and that if you want it enough you can manifest it. You have taken this teaching and put it as "My will be done," over "Thy will be done," and yet it is the same teaching on manifesting. The phrase "Do what thou wilt, an it harm none" is much the same words.

My correspondent's closing reference is from the Wiccan Rede, an ethical code enunciated in 1964 by English wiccan Doreen Valiente who employed elements from Gerald Gardner and Aleister Crowley.

* * *

"People speak of socialism," wrote political theorist Michael Harrington in his 1989 coda *Socialism: Past and Future*. "We should speak of socialisms." The same could be said of Satanism. One-dimensional use of the term, often hitched to self-elevating fantasies of anti-Satanists (who vastly outnumber their imagined targets), is as ridiculous as equating Bernie Sanders and Pol Pot because both are called socialists. Based on personal experience, most anti-Satanists dwell upon lurid accounts of abuse, filled with historical and legal gaps and inventions, in ways I have never witnessed among those they target. I venture that some who collect and brandish these records nurture a prurient interest of their own, perfumed and reprocessed through activist "research."

The most sensational and longest-running case to emerge from the Satanic Panic—and also the longest running in U.S. history—involved California's McMartin Preschool, of which journalist Heather Greene wrote in her 2021 *Lights, Camera, Witchcraft*:

> In 1983, accusations were made against owners and childcare workers at the McMartin Preschool in Manhattan Beach, California. They were accused of ritual child abuse, including sodomy, rape, and other forms of molestation. Stories circulated of animal sacrifice, secret tunnels, blood drinking, the placing of pentagrams on children's bottoms, and more. In 1984, 384 McMartin preschool children of the 400 interviewed were diagnosed as having been sexually abused. Arrests

> were made. Despite all early doubts as to the credibility of the children's testimonies and the legitimacy of various reports, the McMartin trial continued for seven years, becoming the most expensive and longest-running criminal trial in American history.

All charges were dropped in 1990. No one can restore the lives stolen from the falsely accused. Despite repeated historical, legal, and journalistic discrediting, related canards endure in willful suppositions and circumstantial leaps of conspiracy narratives. Implications sometimes emerge on the geopolitical stage. In justifying his attempted annexation of four regions of Ukraine, Vladimir Putin announced in a speech of September 30, 2022, "The repression of freedom is taking on the outlines of a 'reverse religion,' of real Satanism," claiming that Western liberal outlooks amounted to "denial of man." [4]

As alluded, I am attempting to redefine the Satanic in more esoteric terms, according to concepts, principles, and points of view understood by Romantic poets and writers who framed the Satanic current as one of legitimate rebellion, rejection of received concepts, and pursuit of what Crowley termed True Will. Historical and esoteric reading of Satanist metaphysics or philosophy is defensible on those grounds.

Many of us grew up learning the story of humanity's fall from grace in the Biblical parable of the Garden of Paradise. The serpent—long culturally associated with Satan—seduces Eve, and then she Adam, into eating forbidden fruit from the Tree of Knowledge of Good and Evil. This ur-myth appears in the sparsely detailed Genesis 3. When revisiting the formative story, you will find, in virtually any translation, that the serpent's argument is based in truth: the first couple do not perish for eating the apple and their eyes are, in fact, opened to good and evil. Or, as William Blake wrote in another context in *The Marriage of Heaven and Hell*, "the doors of perception were cleansed." Moreover, Eve, contrary to a cultural shibboleth, does not seduce Adam who requires little coaxing. The serpent suggests, as augmented in other texts, that Yahweh displays cruel hypocrisy by forbidding illumination of mind, even as its availability sits in the garden's midst.

It is not clear whether the Tree of Knowledge of Good and Evil and the Tree of Life, both of which appear in Genesis, are two distinct trees or one and the same. One of the earliest exponents of the "one tree" theory was German theologian Karl Budde (1850–1935), followed by Bible scholar Claus Westermann (1909–2000), both traditional figures, widely recognized in the field. What if the Tree of Knowledge of Good and Evil and the Tree of Life are one thing? What kind of life are Adam and Eve conscripted to in paradise without knowledge of good and evil? In such a state, they could not create, compare, produce, and measure. Also true is that they do not know friction. They eat from the tree, they are expelled from Eden, and they beget two sons, Cain and Abel. Differences are introduced into the world. Cain explodes in rage at his brother with whom he has deep fissures. His brother is pious, theological, and favored by God. Cain is independent, a loner and a rebel, and unsuited to worship. Cain loves his brother yet harbors radical differences with him because their parents ate from the Tree of Knowledge of Good and Evil. Cain does something he regrets for the rest of his life. This pathos is reexamined from Cain's perspective in Lord Byron's 1821 closet drama, *Cain*.

Yet if knowledge of good and evil had not been introduced into paradise by the adversarial force, not only would there have been no differences between Cain and Abel but in a very real sense there would have been no Cain and Abel because everything and everyone would be extensions of a certain sameness. There seems no purpose to creation absent distinctions of evaluation and measurement, of production and counter-production, and of friction, which inevitably arises from choice, will, and agency.

Hence, it is possible to view Genesis 3 through a different lens. *It is not a Jewish book or a Christian book*—those are early modern terms—it is, like all primeval mythical works, a parable of human development and selfhood. All great spiritual works emerged from humanity seeking origin and purpose. If we approach Scripture that way, we can detect across history a slender thread of insight that invites new understanding of our foundational Western myth.

I encounter some seekers who embrace my defense of occult or metaphysical practices by which they feel understood but reject any consideration of Satanism because that word for them, as with the word occult in general culture, is so sullied by convention it cannot be revisited. When I began my explorations in 2018, the marketing director of a Manhattan New Age center told me that a "beloved astrologer" threatened to sever ties with the venue unless I canceled or altered the name of a talk on Satanism. I refused and my talk went as planned. The world kept turning.

The last place to look for ethics is in what people say. Any person or organization, particularly of a spiritual or religious bent, can point to strictures and declare, we stand for service or peace or social justice or universal love or some generally meaningless macro-virtue. The Talmudic book *Pirkei Avot* or "Ethics of the Fathers" cautions, "Beware the man who bespeaks his own virtue."

The greatest act of empathy I have experienced in a religious context goes back to when I knelt before a life-sized statue of St. Jude at a Midtown Manhattan Catholic church; I was in agony. As I was walking out, a young man on his knees, probably from Central America, gave me a fist bump. I cannot tell you how much love was in that act. I am not against Catholicism—I love Catholicism. Those who hate or proffer conspiracy theories about Catholicism do so because it contains aspects of the Universal Religion, if there is such thing, and I believe there is.

Contemporaneously, an artist of devotional religious paintings orchestrated a whispering campaign against me that resulted in my being severed from the Association for Research and Enlightenment, or A.R.E., the group dedicated to the teachings of Christian mystic and psychic Edgar Cayce. My talks and writings were erased from organizational media; I was dropped from its prison ministry; a book I wrote gratis as a fundraiser, *Mind As Builder: The Positive-Mind Metaphysics of Edgar Cayce*, was pulled from publication. This is because I am a Romantic Satanist. I have never witnessed an act more bereft of love. It summons a lyric from Jethro Tull's sardonic "Hymn 43":

"If Jesus saves / Well he better save himself / From the gory, glory seekers / Who use his name in death." I have also received private expressions of support from many A.R.E. members for whom I feel deepest warmth. One staffer wrote me, "They may erase you from the website but they cannot erase you from our hearts."

I am working to reform this prejudice. It may be a windmill too great to tilt at; but my effort is underway and you do not turn back once you have embarked on an errand. In a humorous domestic kerfuffle, I was told, "You're not gonna convert Western civilization to Satanism!" Point taken.

Amid such considerations, it may be fairly asked: What about sacrifice for others? What about "giving back?" These things arrive of their own volition, often (more often, I aver) without proclamation or intention. If you realized how many beings underwent sacrifice, suffering, and death for the circumstances that allow you to read these words in material comfort, you would place a different value on your life and what debt you owe for it. I find that most sacrifices, where they actually occur, are intimate and silent. Chapter six explores giving time and money. In matters of giving, harbor no illusions.

There exist a handful of diffuse Satanic organizations, from the foundational and, today, professedly atheistic Church of Satan formed by magickian and artist Anton LaVey (1920–1997) in 1966 (Anton was less cut-and-dried on questions of theism); to the more occultic and spiritual-oriented Temple of Set founded by philosopher and retired officer Michael Aquino (1946–2019); to the activist-driven Satanic Temple, which focuses on First Amendment rights and countering Satanic-Panic fictions. I belong to no group and write as a solitary seeker. Aquino observed that a mark of success in any Satanic organization is that everyone yearns for independence.*

Why piece together an individual Lefthand philosophy? Why not simply embrace Aleister Crowley's *Thelema* ("do what thou wilt . . .") or Ayn Rand's radically capitalistic Objectivism? I deeply respect Thelema and share much with it; but I harbor general aversion to some of the more stringently ceremonial and liturgical expressions of Crowley's thought. This may result, in part, from an orthodox bar mitzvah as a youth, an experience I cherish but do not wish to retread. In any case, I like a statement by philosopher and critic of science Paul Feyerabend: "I am for anarchism in thinking, in one's private life, BUT NOT in public life." [5]

---

* Aquino has been subjected to outrageous falsehood, which I examine in *Modern Occultism* (2023) and "The Trials of Michael Aquino," Substack, May 3, 2025.

Regarding Ayn Rand, I am smitten with her persona, which I consider an act of protean self-creation that represents her greatest work (and compares well to another iconic Russian, Madame H.P. Blavatsky). But I am not in line with philosophical materialism or atheism, which are at the heart of Rand's outlook. I believe we participate in both tactile and extraphysical realms. As I see it, our ancient ancestors were right in identifying and personifying energies or intelligences in nature. I seek relations with a Greater Force.

Recent to this writing, an artist I love, Duncan Trussell (who calls Lucifer "diet Satan"), asked whether there isn't risk in what I am attempting? Especially given mainstream interpretation of the Satanic. I venerate an unprejudiced question, our rarest resource. I abhor rhetorical questions, a device that falsifies this precious means of exchange.

I responded to Duncan's question in two ways. First, religious models—like scientific ones (e.g., string theory, cosmic wormholes)—are just that: models of reality, not reality itself. What we call time is just measurement of time—the thing itself is vastly more elusive. Neither I, nor any seeker, is obligated to abide conceptualizations, no matter how oft repeated. Familiarity is not truth. Never confuse tradition with habit. In light of that, readers may notice paucity of a common word in this discussion: Devil. The Devil is an Old-English term. It is steeped in exoteric prejudices. Beyond proper names or vernacular expressions, I rarely use it. I have been sweetly called a "Devil worshipper." That misses the mark.

But I am not indifferent to larger cultural attitudes. Hence, I must respect the question of risk, which I have asked myself. In short, I determined several years ago that I may be courting risk. I accept that. I privately elected to follow this road as a seeker—I vowed to follow it—and to testify to what is found. That is my self-chosen effort.

If the Lefthand Path possesses an operating principle it is uttered by the Great Rebel of *Paradise Lost*: "Can it be sin to know?" I will never defer to thought systems or customs that forbid the fruit of measurement or punish its consumption.

* * *

An October 5, 2019, *New York Times* column, "How to Sell Your Soul to Donald Trump" by Frank Bruni, referenced the popular legend of medieval wizard Faust pledging to serve Satan in exchange for power and renown. "Selling your soul" to Satan ranks among the most familiar parables in Western culture. But where does it actually come from?

There exist many versions of the Faust drama, most notably by playwright Christopher Marlowe

(1564–1593) and philosopher Johann Wolfgang von Goethe (1749–1832). The latter is widely considered dramatically superior and subtler.

For his part, Marlowe was writing within a backlash against Renaissance occultism. His *Doctor Faustus* is a lyrically beautiful if monochromatic morality tale about the dangers of dabbling in dark forces, for which the protagonist pays with damnation. Goethe's *Faust* is more psychologically and ethically layered. In it, Mephistopheles and Faust circle each other, sharklike, neither quite trusting the other. They finally strike a bargain in which the Dark Lord agrees to grant Faust unbounded happiness and knowledge—with a peculiar catch that binds Mephistopheles to his word: if Faust ever occupies a moment so splendid that he wants to live in it forever only then will he go to his death and vest his soul to Satan. That moment never quite occurs and the sorcerer is saved.

Was there a real Faust? Very likely, but historians have never fully agreed upon who. Rough consensus settled around Johann Georg Faust, a German alchemist, astrologer, theologian, and magickian who died around 1541. Central European legend held that the mysterious figure made a pact with Satan for knowledge and power. This Faust probably formed the model for Marlowe's stage character.

Lots of modern figures are rumored to "sell their souls"—many such stories populate folklore and literature. Baroque violinist Giuseppe Tartini (1692–1770) related one of the most alluring. The composer's famously complex Violin Sonata in G minor, better known as the Devil's Trill Sonata, was, he said, played for him in a dream by Satan. To his agony, Tartini on awakening could reconstruct only a shadow of the original. A similar mythos of Satanic inspiration surrounds the career of violinist Niccolò Paganini (1782–1840), who astounded audiences with his technical prowess and ability to play without sheet music.

In yet another exhibit of Madame Blavatsky's omnipresence, the occultist adapted Tartini's narrative into a short story, "The Ensouled Violin," originally appearing in *The Theosophist* in January 1880 and in her posthumous 1892 collection *Nightmare Tales*. As it must, Blavatsky's horror tale hosts a legend of its own, which is that it was cowritten, along with several other collaborations, by the hidden Cyprian adept called Master Hillarion.

One of the most popular modern iterations of soul selling involves American bluesman Robert Johnson (1911–1938). As popular legend goes, the guitarist met or conjured the devil at a crossroads and vowed to serve him in exchange for preternatural musical skills. Although Johnson recorded a song called "Crossroads," it was not about soul-selling but hitchhiking.

But another blues master, Tommy Johnson (1896–1956), performed a similar—though more elusive—act of magick, recounted by his brother LeDell to biographer David Evans in his 1971 *Tommy Johnson*:

> If you want to learn how to make songs yourself, you take your guitar and you go to where the road crosses that way, where a crossroads is. Get there, be sure to get there just a little 'fore 12 that night so you know you'll be there. You have your guitar and be playing a piece there by yourself . . . A big black man will walk up there and take your guitar and he'll tune it. And then he'll play a piece and hand it back to you. That's the way I learned to play anything I want.

Ledell does not specifically reference Tommy engaging in soul-selling or encountering Satan. Rather, Tommy drew upon a practice found in the Black magickal tradition of hoodoo. Due to phonetic and cultural intersections, hoodoo is sometimes confused with Vodou. Vodou is an Afro-Caribbean religion with its own deities, priesthood, and liturgy, properly spelled Vodou in Haiti and Voodoo in the American South. The term hoodoo is lowercase. Its etymology is unclear. But hoodoo may come from *huduba,* used among the Hausa people of West and Central Africa meaning to arouse resentment against someone. In blues songs, singers sometimes lament being "hoodooed"—i.e., crossed and tricked by spell casting. Hoodoo was and remains a syncretic, spell-working system originated by enslaved people in the U.S. Within the framework of hoodoo, Tommy, at least in his brother's account, was practicing a retention of Western and Central African magick in which a seeker summons a deific protector, sometimes in the form of Ellegua or Eshu, who guards the crossroads and dispenses wisdom and artistry, similar to the Hellenic god Hermes or Mercury.

A sketchy but intriguing online legend has Bob Dylan following Tommy Johnson's footsteps and selling his soul to Satan for fame and artistry, at least according to his elliptical (and fascinating) 2004 interview on *60 Minutes*:

Ed Bradley: Why do you still do it? Why are you still out here?

Dylan: Well it goes back to the destiny thing. I made a bargain with it, you know, a long time ago and I'm holding up my end.

Bradley: What was your bargain?

Dylan: To get where I am now.

Bradley: [laughing] Should I ask who you made the bargain with?

Dylan: With, you know, with the chief commander.
Bradley: On this earth?
Dylan: On this earth and in the world we can't see.

This is, of course, a shaky interpretation. But Dylan, the perennial trickster (in the mold of Hermes and Eshu), won't let on for sure.

Where, finally, does the idea of selling your soul to Satan originate from, at least in the Western mind? The likeliest and earliest source is the Old Testament book Isaiah 28:15, in which nonbelievers are said to elude bad tidings by striking a deal with nether-forces. It appears this way in a 1985 translation by the Jewish Publication Society (JPS):

> For you have said, "We have made a covenant with Death, Concluded a pact with Sheol. When the sweeping flood passes through, It shall not reach us; For we have made falsehood our refuge, Taken shelter in treachery."

Sheol references the Hebrew concept of the afterworld—sometimes translated *netherworld* as in JPS's 1917 translation—and is not synonymous with more modern concepts of Hell, the term used in the King James Bible. Although notions of a personified Satan had not fully taken shape in the Biblical era, the idea of a maleficent pact spread among early Christians and probably formed the basis of "selling your soul."

As a historian and participant in occult and esoteric movements, I never dodge the all-important question: does it work? Well, I have provided background and tools. If this book possesses a guiding principle, it is: never permit past convention to curb current experiment. If your spiritual journey involves a relationship to some personified energy, from whatever time, place, or culture, I offer this observation: It could be that deity does not afford you favors but grants you the strength to attain favors. Or favors themselves may also come. Are you prepared for them? I prescribe no medicine I have not taken myself.

* * *

In closing, I know that some reading these words may find, as I once did, that their search seems at a dead end. They feel that they have cycled-out or failed to reach a wished-for destination.

Allow me a tangent: It seems to me that art is expression that plants new ideas in its witness. I was inspired this way seeing a production of Japanese underground theater maestro Shuji Terayama's play *Duke Bluebeard's Castle* at the Japan Society in New York. (I have also experienced this with the work of musical expressionist Geneva Jacuzzi.) As I viewed Terayama's play, I realized how to end this study—with a prayer of salutation for any who wish to use it. This address can precede your petition:

God of Wishes Fulfilled
God of the Outsiders
God of Reciprocity
God of Retribution
Grant what I ask
Which I am prepared to pay for

Remember: in some cases, payment has already been made—and the ask is earned.

Notes

[1] "Reaching Nietzschean Individualists" in *Encountering New Religious Movements* edited by Irving Hexham, Stephen Rost & John W. Moorhead II (Kregel, 2004)

[2] E.g., see "It's Time to Revisit the Satanic Panic" by Alan Yuhas, *New York Times*, March 31, 2021; "I'm Sorry" [the recantation of a former child witness] by Kyle Zirpolpo as told to Debbie Nathan, *Los Angeles Times*, October 30, 2005; "Why Satanic Panic never really ended" by Aja Romano, *Vox*, March 31, 2021, and "The McMartin Preschool

Abuse Trial: An Account" by Douglas O. Linder at Famous-Trails.com. I consider the matter further in *Modern Occultism* (2023).

[3] *Plutarch Lives*, Vol. VII, Loeb Classical Library, translated by Bernadotte Perrin, Harvard University Press, 1919

[4] "Putin's speech on annexation paints a stark picture of a face-off with the West" by Anton Troianovski, *New York Times*, September 30, 2022

[5] *Against Method*, fourth edition, by Paul Feyerabend (Verso, 1975, 1988, 1993, 2010)

FIFTEEN

"My Name Is Called Disturbance"

"What is simple is typically made out to be obscure . . ."

—Hegel, 1810 [1]

I vowed in this book to interrogate accepted religious forms. As I see it, the problem with religion is one of simplicity. Initial experience and insight—sometimes ensconced deep in antiquity and other times occurring through modern habits—are codified into strictures, concepts, and laws.

The same process plays out in breakaway, reformist, or alternative movements initially founded to elude this reification.

My effort in *Esoterika* is to consider—using admittedly fragmentary forms that have reached us—what extra-physical ideas and contacts meant to humanity's deep-ancient ancestry prior to centuries-long, sometimes millennia-long, conditioning, social filters, and redefinition, resulting in what most contemporary people consider the traditions.

This chapter deepens query into the most controversial religious subject in Western life: the presence and meaning of Satan and, indirectly, of Satanism, a modern concept, as an independent path. My intent is not practical in any direct sense; it is heretical in the highest iteration of that term: thought that departs—using visible weights and measures—from the given. If I clarify something for you, let that clarity be expressed in your search.

The Disturber

My exploration opens with an observation, easily overlooked, by controversial Jewish scholar Friedrich Weinreb (1910–1988). In his 1963 exegesis *Roots of the Bible*, Weinreb observes: "The word Satan really means 'disturber' . . ." [2]

As noted, the earliest Abrahamic concept of Satan is rooted in the Hebrew השטן (*ha-sa-taan*), literally "The Satan" or the adversary (sometimes the prosecutor or opposer), or the Latin-derived term Lucifer, or light bringer (originally a condemnation of the ancient king of Babylon as a falling star in Isaiah 14:12). Weinreb's definition is *sui generis* but entirely defensible.

He further notes:

> One can *oneself* be a god, fix standards for oneself, decide for oneself on life and death, on development or stagnation. It is for this reason, according to ancient lore, when they [Abraham and Isaac] were on their way to Moria, Satan advanced towards them.

Weinreb's considered term "ancient lore" is where we begin digging. Nowhere in Genesis 22 does Satan appear or attempt to intervene when Abraham, under command of Yahweh, takes his only son Isaac to Mount Moriah to be sacrificed.

A deeper and more heterodox narrative of the Disturber's intervention appears in works of Rabbinic and Talmudic commentary—and a debated "lost book" of the Hebrew Bible. Within this "underground history" resides a deeper and fuller texture of the ur-myth on which Western modernity stands.

Three Days Unknown

"Centuries ago," writes twenty-first-century scholar of Jewish folklore Eli Yassif, "sages and preachers tried to 'fill' the gaps in the Biblical story of Isaac's near-sacrifice. The largest of the gaps lies between two sentences that dryly describe Abraham and Isaac's journey to the site of the sacrifice." [3]

Yassif continues:

> What happened during those three fateful days? Is it possible that nothing happened between the father and his son being led to sacrifice? Is it possible that Isaac did not utter a word, or grimace? Did the father not twinge with doubt as he set out, or display grief about the impending loss of his beloved boy?

Several possibilities exist. The most controversial source for discerning the "in between" days in Genesis 22 is a confounding work, at least twice seemingly referenced in Scripture, and emerging with arguable legitimacy during the late Renaissance, *Sefer Hayashar* or *The Book of the Righteous*. Before considering the apocryphal book, I rely upon more traditional Talmudic and Rabbinic scholarship.

As is widely known, Abraham is tested in his loyalty when asked to sacrifice his only son, thirty-seven-year-old Isaac. The elderly patriarch is unlikely to bear another. Even facing such tragedy, the forefather prepares to give everything—only to be stayed at the last moment by an angelic hand. The story has generated massive existential controversy. As a child raised in conservative and orthodox synagogues, I recall my older sister, Nina, objecting to the test. Satan agrees with Nina.

Within the Babylonian Talmud tract Midrash Tanchuma, Vayera 22, passages 9–12, appears a little-known encounter between Satan, Abraham, and Isaac on the trek to Mount Moriah, site of Isaac's intended death. Satan stops Abraham and asks what he is doing:

> Satan appeared before him on the road in the guise of an old man and asked: "Whither are you going?" Abraham replied: "To pray." "And why," Satan retorted, "does one going to pray carry fire and a knife in his hands, and wood on his shoulders?"*

Abraham, perhaps wishing to thwart the unknown interloper, lies to him. Satan sees through the lie. "The *satan* in the Hebrew Bible never lies," observes Esther J. Hamori, professor of Hebrew Bible at Union Theological Seminary. [4] Satan challenges Abraham:

> Why should an old man, who begets a son at the age of a hundred, destroy him? Have you not heard the parable of the man who destroyed his own possessions and then was forced to beg from others?

---

* https://www.sefaria.org/Midrash_Tanchuma%2C_Vayera.22.10?lang=bi&with=About&lang2=en

Abraham insists that he is only following the word of God. Seeing that the elder is unreachable, Satan moves on to Isaac:

> Satan departed from him and appeared at Isaac's right hand in the guise of a youth. He inquired: "Where are you going?" "To study the law," Isaac replied. "Alive or dead?" he retorted. "Is it possible for a man to learn the law after he is dead?" Isaac queried. He said to him: "Oh, unfortunate son of an unhappy mother, many days your mother fasted before your birth, and now this demented old man is about to sacrifice you." Isaac replied: "Even so, I will not disregard the will of my Creator, nor the command of my father."

In his last-ditch effort, the Disturber on the third day conjures a river to block the path of the father-son—but with God's help the barrier dries up and they reach their destination. The conventional reading of the story posits Satan as disrupter of God's will—or more likely an agent of it—common themes in Jewish Scripture, commencing with Satan's conflation—both in Rabbinic commentary and later cultural archetype—with the serpent in the garden. But conventional readings are often tone-deaf to deeper considerations, as probed in the Talmudic tract.

When revisiting the familiar framing of the serpent in Genesis 3, virtually any translation demonstrates that not only is the serpent's argument basically true—the couple does not die for eating the apple, and their eyes are, in fact, opened to good and evil (as noted, some scholars contend that the garden's two trees, the Tree of Knowledge of Good and Evil and the Tree of Life, are the same)—but also that Eve, contrary to a canard of female nature, does not trick Adam, who requires little convincing. The serpent even suggests, as augmented in other texts, that Yahweh demonstrates hypocrisy by forbidding intellectual illumination, even as its availability sits within paradise.

As magickal scholar Damien Echols has written of the garden: "The same division that created suffering also makes freedom possible . . . The eating of the fruit wasn't the end. It was the first breath of the Great Work." [5]

"Comely and Well Favored"

Having considered the three "lost days" from a Talmudic perspective, I now turn to a more unconventional—but no less intriguing—source, the apocryphal *Sefer Hayashar* itself.

Chapter twenty-three of the contested book retells the Abraham-Isaac-Satan story, but with a more erotic quality when Satan confronts Isaac:

> And Satan returned and came to Isaac; and he appeared unto Isaac in the figure of a young man comely and well favored. And he approached Isaac and said unto him, Dost thou not know and understand that thy old silly father bringeth thee to the slaughter this day for naught? Now therefore, my son, do not listen nor attend to him, for he is a silly old man, and let not thy precious soul and beautiful figure be lost from the earth. [6]

Again, son and father push past the intruder.

Sefer Hayashar is (arguably) noted twice in Scripture and forms the subject of fitful debate in the Talmud, as noted by independent (some would say heterodox) scholar James Scott Trimm: "The Talmud discusses the identity of Jasher but also fails to offer us much real direction. In b.Avodah Zarah 25a several theories for the identity of the Book of Jasher are proposed." [7]

Trimm further notes historical corroboration of such an ancient book by Roman-Jewish historian Flavius Josephus (c. 37–c. 100 A.D.):

> In his own recounting of the event of the prolonged day of Yahushua [Joshua] 10 the first century Jewish Roman historian Josephus identifies the Book of Jasher mentioned by Yahushua as one of "the books laid up in the Temple" ([*Antiquities of the Jews*] 5:1:17). Thus the Book of Jasher was known to Josephus and was known to be among the books laid up in the Temple in the first century.

At least two direct references—and one further debated reference—to *Sefer Hayashar* appear in the Bible. Joshua 10:13 states:

> And the Sun stood still, and the Moon stayed, until the people had avenged themselves on their enemies. Is this not written in *Sefer HaYashar*? [8]

2 Samuel 1:18 states:

> To teach the sons of Judah [the use of] the bow. Behold, it is written in the book of Jasher.

A third—and questionable—allusion may appear in 1 Kings 8.

The first two references appear to confirm the "lost book" as a work of authentic Biblical vintage. But contention swirls. Medieval Jewish sage Rashi (c. 1040–1105)—who commands canonical authority—suggests that the Joshua and Samuel passages may refer more generally to the Book of Genesis in the Septuagint, the earliest Greek translation of Jewish Scripture.

Hence, there is question over whether the Biblical references to *Sefer Hayashar* stand up. Just as there is debate over whether *Sefer Hayashar* is properly considered a "lost book" at all or is, rather, simply a commentary produced in its earliest form in Hebrew in 1625 in Venice. The 1887 English translation from which I quote, issued by Salt Lake City publisher J. H. Parry & Company, uses the date 1613.

There is no settling this debate. But the alternate narrative I highlight possesses undeniable historical context based on Talmudic sources alone.

Leavening Satan

There exists no evidence—at least none I have found—of a schismatic cult of *ha-sa-taan* veneration among ancient Jews. That said, it bears noting that ancient Judaism was not exclusively monotheistic.

"Previous studies of theophoric [God-bearing] names," writes historian and journalist Ariel David, "have already given support to the widespread scholarly conclusion that the ancient Hebrews, particularly in the Kingdom of Israel, were far from strict monotheists, as YHWH [or Yahweh] was only one of several tutelary deities who was attached to baby names." [9]

Ancient Jews in Northern Israel—like "pagans" or backwater villagers in the Roman Empire—tended more toward polytheism than their more traditionally situated countrymen. Across generations, this changed and monotheism grew more the norm. In the Babylonian Talmudic tract Bava Bathra ("The Last Gate") 16a, passage 9, appears this leavening note about Satan expressing gratitude toward the prophet Samuel: "Rav Aḥa bar Ya'akov taught this in Paphunya [a town of Babylonia], and *Satan came and kissed his feet in gratitude for speaking positively about him.*" [emphasis added] Those interested in petitionary spirituality, take note.

Bava Batra 16a

The William Davidson Talmud (Koren - Steinsaltz)

אָמַר רַבִּי לֵוִי: שָׂטָן וּפְנִינָּה לְשֵׁם שָׁמַיִם נִתְכַּוְּונוּ. שָׂטָן – כֵּיוָן דַּחֲזָיֵא לְהַקָּדוֹשׁ בָּרוּךְ הוּא דְּנָטְיָה דַּעְתֵּיהּ בָּתַר אִיּוֹב, אָמַר: חַס וְשָׁלוֹם מִינַּשֵּׁי לֵיהּ לְרַחְמָנוּתֵיהּ דְּאַבְרָהָם. פְּנִינָּה – דִּכְתִיב: "וְכִעֲסַתָּה צָרָתָהּ גַּם כַּעַס, בַּעֲבוּר הַרְּעִימָהּ". דַּרְשַׁהּ רַב אַחָא בַּר יַעֲקֹב בְּפַפּוּנְיָא. אֲתָא שָׂטָן, נַשְּׁקֵיהּ לְכַרְעֵיהּ.

Rabbi Levi says: Both **Satan,** who brought accusations against Job, **and Peninnah,** who tormented Hannah, mother of Samuel the prophet, acted with **intent** that was **for the sake of Heaven.** As for **Satan, when he saw that the Holy One, Blessed be He, inclined to** favor **Job** and praised him, **he said: Heaven forbid that He should forget the love of Abraham.** With regard to **Peninnah, as it is written: "And her rival wife also provoked her sore, to make her fret"** (**I Samuel 1:6**), i.e., Peninnah upset Hannah in order to motivate her to pray. **Rav Aḥa bar Ya'akov taught** this **in Paphunya,** and **Satan came and kissed his feet** in gratitude for speaking positively about him.

"Even Satan appreciated human recognition and was properly grateful for it," write historians Hershey H. Friedman, Ph.D., and Steve Lipman in their 1999 paper, "Satan the Accuser: Trickster in Talmudic and Midrashic Literature." [10]

Again, Friedman and Lipman:

> In the Talmud (Avodah Zarah 20b), Shmuel's father quotes the Angel of Death [Samael, often conflated with Satan] as saying: "If I did not care for the dignity of human beings, I would cut open the throat of man as [wide and gaping as] that of a slaughtered animal." In other words, Satan prefers using the poison on the tip of his sword rather than the sword itself to kill mortals because he does not feel that people should be mutilated by death.

Here we see Satan not exactly as humanist—but certainly a different kind of historical figure than is traditionally understood.

Bible scholar Hamori goes further: "If one can avoid transposing a later Christian image onto the character in the Hebrew Bible, one might even call him . . . admirable." (The ellipses are not mine but appear in her original.)

"Archangel of Legitimate Resolution"

The literary-spiritual-esoteric journey I describe—of Satan not as force of evil but as disturber and questioner—continued, most notably and fatefully, in the work of John Milton who drew not from Rabbinic or apocryphal sources but the ambiguous and spare Genesis 3, along with a few other fragments referencing Satan in Scripture, and constructed his unparalleled *Paradise Lost*, which forever disrupted the image of Lucifer in the Western mind.

In Milton's work, the monarch of fearful depravity—so culturally conditioned centuries later—is restored to a figure of defiant and even laudable rebellion, at least in the opening chapters, particularly books one and two. Milton's epic presents the Dread Rebel, who is unbowed following his defeat and ejection from heaven, as a diabolical optimist: "The mind is its own place, and in it self / Can make a Heav'n of Hell, a Hell of Heav'n." Satan's minions mirror his formidability. The demon Mammon at one point declares, "Hard liberty before the easy yoke."

I will share a secret. Once upon a time, I was friends with political organizer-agitator Steve Bannon. No more. I could not stomach election denialism. After Steve got ejected from the White House during

Trump's first term, I messaged him the "hard liberty" quote just cited. His reply: "Dude!!!!!!!!!!!!!" Indeed.

Like Milton, visionary poet-mystic William Blake blew open the Western imagination in 1790 with his verse portfolio *The Marriage of Heaven and Hell*, in which he made the incendiary observation: "One Law for the Lion & Ox is Oppression." Blake, you might say, gave the devil his due by positing the offending figure as a necessary counterpart to narrowly dogmatic virtue. Blake's "Proverbs of Hell" are particularly affecting, and filled with layered observations, such as: "All wholesome food is caught without a net or a trap."

Blake's entry into the Western literary and ethical mind left a profound impact on the rising generation of Romantic writers and philosophers, including Percy Bysshe and Mary Wollstonecraft Shelley (1797–1851) and Lord Byron, who sharpened the image of Lucifer as misunderstood radical.

I alluded earlier to perhaps the most alluring and underappreciated work to emerge from "Romantic Satanism": Lord Byron's 1821 drama, *Cain*, which I consider the most jarring literary reconception of Lucifer next to Milton's.

Byron's Satan, who befriends the rebellious and ill-fated Cain, is persuasive and penetrating in his denial that he was the serpent in the garden and in pointing out that the serpent greeted Eve as a sexual and political emancipator—an outlook embraced by many proto-feminists and political radicals of that century and the next.

Like Milton's Satan, Byron's Dark Lord is a fiery optimist and something of a socialist, who tells Cain, "I know the thoughts / Of dust, and feel for it, and with you." Of course, the play ends with Cain's tragic and unintended act of fratricide, leaving the reader to wonder: Are competing ideologies and human frictions the inevitable cost of awareness?

Many proto-feminists in the nineteenth century, and others during the Romantic age, did, in fact—as artists, rebels, and political agitators—view Satan as a kind of philosophical grandfather. They saw not-quite-metaphorical Satan in league with certain readings in Romantic, anarchist, and socialist literature, not as the enemy of humanity but its rough liberator. [11]

In matters of the Satanic, Romantic and esoteric Jewish views are not in opposition. Again, historians Friedman and Lipman: "John Milton, in *Paradise Lost*, has Satan saying: 'Better to reign in hell than serve in heaven.' From what we see of the Satan described in the Talmud and Midrash, he is not all that interested in being of the ruling elite. He revels in his work as a tempter of mankind, a tester of the righteous . . . He is a trickster *par excellence*."

The mythos I have traced appears esoterically in modern Western letters, fostering statements from the mouth of Satan like this one in the serialized novel *Consuelo* (1842–1843) by "George Sand," popular byline of France's covert woman of letters Amantine Lucile Aurore Dupin de Francueil. Satan appears in a vision to the novel's heroine, intoning:

> my brother Christ loved you not better than I love you. It is time that you should know me, and that in lieu of calling me the enemy of the human race, you recover in me the friend who has aided you through the great struggle. I am not the demon. I am the archangel of legitimate resolution . . .

This is the voice below the floorboards (or locked in the attic) of Western life. It is a voice that cannot be contained—because it forever whispers, *look for yourself.* Or, once more, as Milton's Satan puts it: "Can it be sin to know?"

"My Name Is Called Disturbance"

What, finally, about the quotation in my chapter title? It has a story of its own on which I close.

For years, like many Westerners of my generation, I have loved the 1968 Rolling Stones song "Street Fighting Man." Recent to this writing, I discovered a cover by Ace Frehley and, perhaps because Ace enunciates differently from Mick, I picked up a lyric I had never before deciphered:

> Hey, said *my name is called Disturbance*
> I'll shout and scream, I'll kill the king
> I'll rail at all his servants

The phrase would not leave me. Days after hearing it, with no indication why, I plucked from my shelf an unread copy of Weinreb's *Roots of the Bible*—and began my journey.

Thank you Mick and Keith for reading the ether, as one might say, "At Her Satanic Majesty's Request."

Notes

[1] Hegel is quoted from a comment on Mesmerism (notable in itself) in a letter of October 15, 1810, to P.G. van Ghert (1782–1852), a student and later friend:

> It is precisely the simplicity of animal magnetism which I hold to be most noteworthy. For what is simple is typically made out to be obscure . . . Its operation seems to consist in the sympathy into

which one animal organism [Individualität] is capable of entering with a second . . . That [sympathetic] union [of two organisms] leads life back again into its pervasive universal stream.

From *Hegel: The Letters* translated by Clark Butler and Christiane Seiler (Indiana University Press, 1984)

[2] Weinreb's study first appeared in Dutch in 1963 and in English in 2021 with Angelico Press, a Catholic scholarly publisher. The fairest brief assessment I know of Weinreb's career—which included the repugnant cloud of his collaborating with the Nazis and sacrificing the lives of his own people—appears at: https://www.jewishvirtuallibrary.org/weinreb-friedrich. As of this writing, I have not fully researched the charges against Weinreb but intend to return to this point.

[3] "Satanic Verses: An apocryphal tale tells of the inner conversation Isaac had with the devil en route to his near-sacrifice" by Eli Yassif, *Haaretz*, September 17, 2010

[4] "Before the *satan* Was Evil" by Esther J. Hamori in *Evil: A History* edited by Andrew P. Chignell (Oxford Philosophical Concepts, 2019). In the Kindle edition of this anthology, Hamori's byline is mistakenly (and, in my view, unconscionably) mis-

spelled as Hamorip. In my twenty-seven years in trade publishing, I never permitted misspelling of a byline.

[5] "The Garden of Eden: An alchemical reading of the Fall" by Damien Echols, Substack, August 6, 2025

[6] I quote from the 1887 English translation issued by Salt Lake City publisher J.H. Parry & Company. This translation is also used by Yassif.

[7] I quote Trimm from his 2008 introduction to a reissue of *Sefer Hayashar*: "The 'Book of Jasher' presented in this volume was published in Hebrew in Venice in 1625, translated into English by Mosheh Samuel and published by Mordechai Noah in New York in 1840. It was Mosheh Samuel who first divided the work into chapter and verse (being 91 chapters). A second edition of this translation was published in Salt Lake City by J. H. Parry & Company in 1887." There also exists a spurious *Book of Jasher*, published 1750 in which the title is deemed the name of its author.

[8] Translation here and below is from mechon-mamre .org

[9] "Names Reveal Unseen History of Biblical Kingdoms of Israel and Judah, Researchers Say" by Ariel David, *Haaretz*, May 12, 2025

[10] "Satan the Accuser: Trickster in Talmudic and Midrashic Literature" by Hershey H. Friedman,

Ph.D., and Steve Lipman, *Thalia: Studies in Literary Humor*, Vol. 18, March 1999

[11] Useful and compelling overviews appear in *Satanic Feminism* by Per Faxneld (Oxford University Press, 2014) and *The Devil's Party: Satanism in Modernity* edited by Per Faxneld and Jesper Aa. Petersen (Oxford University Press, 2012).

SIXTEEN

It Is Not Getting Better

I have been plain about my search. I now proceed—more broadly—from a place of self-disclosure. Not total disclosure—because I think none of us can, or necessarily should, do that. But exceptional.

I do so not to be morbidly revealing, in which I take no pleasure. My aim is to state with urgency and possibility something that may help those of us who seek self-development through esoteric, mythical, and spiritual paths.

G.I. Gurdjieff said, "The past controls the future but the present controls the past." Vernon Howard said something similar to the effect that changing your life now runs backwards (and hence forwards) and necessarily alters your entire existence.

Good to be Bad

The habits that we carry in life are perniciously organic.

They are pleasurable even in their destructiveness.

For me, one such pleasure is anger.

I recall as vividly as the words I am writing that at age four I used to walk on a yellow bus heading to a summer camp clenching my fists and saying, "Rats, rats . . ." Some of the older kids found it cute and funny. And I was, to an extent, self-consciously performative. But watching my father, who had problems enough of his own, I saw anger as a way that a man proved power. Archie Bunker was, for me, not just a tragic (if heartful) hero but actually a model of how a man is supposed to be.

Moreover, there was—and remains—in the expression of anger a pleasure.

Do not dare tell yourself that whatever traits you wish to be rid of do not also contain pleasure. Because we humans are selfish and rarely repeat things without pleasure—or, in remarkable cases, a goal in mind.

Gurdjieff compared emotions to a horse. They kick and cannot be controlled. The danger of a horse is not only its physical might but its absence of intellect in dealing with emotions—especially when those emotions, sometimes negative, are driven by pleasure.

My horse, perhaps like yours, has an arrow in its side. The arrow is what comes from the powerlessness and humiliation born of frustrated emotions. I may have, and, shamefully, still do, consider anger power. But I was once weaker than other horses and the agony of that drove an arrow into my side. It is as innate to my being as a limb.

That arrow is never going to get shaken out.

We are told that ephemeral things in life do not matter. I am not so sure. The arrow is not coming out. So, I venture it is worth watching very carefully for those things and relationships in life that evoke joy. Those are not trinkets or baubles. That is a mistake of imported values. They are as real as whatever drove the arrow into my—and your—side. Be aware of them.

The negative traits that make the horse kick are killing you. I know this to be true because I write these words following decades of search, and I cannot imagine that my life, or any life, is exceptional. This is why we enjoy (or suffer) universal experiences.

Do not fool yourself that intellect can remove the arrow. The intellect—or, in Gurdjieff's metaphor, the carriage driver—cannot communicate with the horse. There exist no reins. How do we get reins? Through what Gurdjieff called "conscious suffering"—self-remembering (a near-impossibility), burying my preferences (at least in petty matters), and what he termed "intentionally made being-efforts." For the latter, you might consider the routines of a traditional martial artist or yogi. That creates a substance referenced in his masterpiece *Beelzebub's Tales to His Grandson* as *Hanbledzoïn*. I do not know whether this substance, with the term blood rooted in it, is real any more than I know whether routine terms like "soul" or "spirit" are real. But for our sake they had better be.

Knowing that the horse cannot be controlled—and if you do not know that you will learn through decades of tuition—it falls to you, the hapless driver, to observe. That is available to us. Observation is, in itself, an organizing principle. If you neglect it, you neglect your life.

Resolutions from an easy chair are worthless. But death has a way of focusing a small few of us. Be among that small few. The being-efforts and observations you make today, if done with sincerity, do, I believe—and esoteric wisdom also dictates—have capacity to change your existence just as a fungus introduced into a root network is untraceably vast in impact.

"There Is No Time"

After a week at the Monroe Institute, two friends of mine hit the road and stopped at a diner. They wrote over the sign posting the hours, "There Is No Time."

They were correct. (The angry owner can send me the bill.) The "arrow of time" is a nineteenth-century materialist concept. Proofs abound in quantum mechanics, both mathematically and materially, that time moves backwards. This occurs, of course, at the subatomic particle level. Cornell research psychologist Daryl J. Bem has recently provided replicated, parsed evidence—proven confirmatory in a meta-analysis encompassing ninety experiments (including his originals) in thirty-three distinct labs in fourteen different nations—that this occurs cognitively as well.* In short, the present unfolds with, not apart from, the future. "The past controls the future but the present controls the past." Take that with deadly seriousness.

There may be times in life where you must take a stand. When I was the same age that I clenched my fists saying "rats," I had the most vivid dream of my life. In our neighborhood in Queens lived a girl, Eleanor, who was deaf. When she spoke the words came out like the high-pitched squeal of a radio frequency. No one could understand her. Kids would laugh and run away. I cannot imagine the silent agony this must have been.

---

* REVISED: Feeling the future: A meta-analysis of 90 experiments on the anomalous anticipation of random future events" [version 2; peer review: 2 approved] by Daryl Bem, Patrizio E. Tressoldi, Thomas Rabeyron, Michael Duggan, first published: 30 Oct 2015, latest published: 29 Jan 2016, last updated: 23 Jul 2020, *F1000Research*

I dreamed that some bad men had kidnapped Eleanor. A circle of my friends gathered and I announced: "We gotta save Eleanor."

It is easy to get lost in sentimentality. I may not be strong enough to save Eleanor. But by saving self a fragment goes toward saving her. Do you see this? Try.

Save Money

Whatever habits are killing you—mine is anger—observe the pleasure that arises from them. See the impossibility of the arrow growing dislodged (and, generally speaking, save yourself copious sums of money on rerunning your week in talk therapy—money that can go towards beauty, education, home, child-raising, and travel). Realize—in humanity's only hope—the encroachment of death for everyone you lay eyes on, and for yourself. See the impending death of others versus your own. It is easier. We are hypnotized (another story entirely) to regard our death with obliviousness. And then observe.

Do you think time is limitless? I do too. It is not. In January 2019 I took my younger son to visit my mother at a luxury high-rise in Queens. I find most of the residents—elderly, well-off, childish, grabby, rude—disgusting. Her behavior, I will spare the details, was typically abhorrent. I pled with her, like an idiot prophet, to leaven certain things, small things, that caused pain. She grinned. It was the last time I saw her in health.

We do not want change. We want relief from suffering. We enjoy the thing that causes suffering. Such as making others suffer—the pleasure of the bully / victim, both of whom dwell in *one person* like a DNA strand.

The past is as real—right now—as the words you are reading. Your efforts today will change that past. And with it, everything.

Do not reach for some polished, holy quotation to find "other words" for what you are receiving. It is not *like* anything. It is truth. Try.

SEVENTEEN

The Day My Search Changed

This is a chapter I never expected to write. I have changed my mind about a central element of spiritual and ethical practice.

First, some background. My teacher, now deceased, was a Harvard-trained physician who, when young, faced a crossroads. He was unsure whether to prioritize a medical career or the search. He selected the search.

The conundrum, he said, was settled for him by the passage from Matthew 6:33: "Seek first the kingdom of God and his righteousness, and all these things will be added to you."

This passage is rooted in 1 Kings 3:10–13, where Yahweh tells Solomon that since he asked for wisdom, he would receive not only that but "I will give you what you have not asked for—both wealth and honor—so that in your lifetime you will have no equal among kings."

For my teacher, these passages resolved his dilemma. I was unsure he had made the right choice. He had suffered grief and want later in life. Would any of it had occurred differently had he prioritized his profession? I do not know. Had he chosen differently I might well have never become his student. Still, my choice differed from his.

I began to rethink this recently after a series of back-to-back podcasts with occultist Sanhre Daffowt. In part two, Sanhre remarked: "I would say if you want to manifest love into your life, the correct and the fastest way to do that is to work on making yourself into the ideal partner for the partner that you want."

Sanhre observed that in spell work or setting of intention one must ask whether I am personally suited for the support and fostering of what is sought. Am I capable of managing and holding the wished-for thing, such as a relationship or better job? Rather than request the thing or circumstance, ask, *really ask*, for the ability to warrant, hold, and have the thing or circumstance. That assumes payment.

In matters of mind metaphysics and selection, I began to work with Sanhre's idea. I began asking for the characterological fiber—perhaps physical and extra-physical—to foster and sustain the thing or circumstance sought.

As I did this, a remarkable opportunity reached me. I asked an aforementioned friend, Bob Roth, executive director of the David Lynch Foundation, whether I might interview Dr. Tony Nader, M.D., Ph.D., successor to Maharishi Mahesh Yogi and head of the worldwide TM movement. Dr. Nader lives in Paris. I asked Bobby on September 1, 2025. As happens in his world, which teems with remarkable occurrences, I had lunch in New York City with Dr. Nader—a privilege of my life—on September 10, 2025.

A portion of our interview touched—indirectly and unintentionally—on a macro version of what I had been considering. Its full relevance on a personal scale did not occur to me until afterward:

> **Mitch**: I have a historical question for you. It seems to me that the search for ultimate principles here in the West may have gotten disrupted in the mid-to-late nineteenth century when Marx, and I'm speaking colloquially, of course, decided that Hegel needed to be flipped and that we needed to get rid of what he derisively called all the mysticism in Hegel, and he said, in effect, "let's get down to economics." So he flipped Hegel and that was persuasive to many people. That remains persua-

sive in greater or lesser degree today, including among people who have never heard of Hegel and will never read a page of Hegel. They are persuaded that the real ebb and flow of life is money and resources versus consciousness. I think Hegel would have agreed with every word you're saying. He felt that on a level of ideas, which he defined metaphysically, if I can use that word, there exists friction, and eventually one idea carries the day. And it continues until another idea carries the day. And he believed that ideas or consciousness are all there is. He used the word idea or *Idee* in German. You and others use the term consciousness, but it's the same conversation. It seems a terrible misfortune for the West. That's my point of view. I don't know if you want to comment on Hegel.

Dr. Nader: Yes, it's similar. It's really, once again, the same story of reality: is it money or consciousness? Money or economics are expressions of consciousness, which we don't shy away from. And the reality is that one can find this outcome of two contradictory things that Hegel calls the outcome of what he terms the dialectic. And money is a means. The problem is, if you reject one or the other, you get into trouble. If you reject consciousness, you lose the priority, because you live life through your consciousness. How can you reject consciousness? You can have all the money in the world but you can be depressed and you have anxieties and fears, even about your money. And you live that. Then what's the meaning of it? And if you go and leave life, which for a while India did, which is the ideal of being only consciousness and meditating, not being practical and in life, then you don't achieve even the enjoyments of life that are offered through consciousness. The dialectic is real, yes. So that's why we call it 200% of life. 100% of being and consciousness and then 100% of enjoyment and relative life. But not excessive in either case. You know, if you go into the excess in one and say, "Oh, this is what my senses want, this is what I get enjoyment from"—and you forget the basic, which is consciousness, which is goodness, which is all the other values, then you become a slave of money, not an owner of the money. You become owned by the money. So, it's not a question of possessing money. It's a question of being possessed by money. So this is how you lose priorities. Then there is no more dialectic, there is no more coming together of opposite forces—or that seem opposite, and that's the problem. It's like East and West. East is maybe at one time spiritual and conscious. West is material and all of that. And of course, West, at

> one time was thinking no one wanted to be spiritual. The West wanted material values. But then it forgot the value of consciousness and spirituality and just got drawn in by materiality and all of that. So it almost became more material, in a way, than Marx is.

Bringing this down to a personal scale, I had been doing intimately what I perceived Marx doing historically: reversing the order of life. I sought the *condition* that I trusted would bring happiness—before seeking the *developed state* or consciousness that would hold and foster, and, hence, make possible, the condition.

Now, let me add a clarifying note. Nothing I suggest here should imply my embrace of another's path or language, historically or personally. My path remains protean. My aim is adjusted to reflect *source* versus *result*. This change is still too fresh and tender to announce it explicitly. But I offer you the paradigm. Your aim must be strictly and solely your own, or it is recitation. Let nothing dissuade you from that. But—ask yourself: are you focused on foundation or structure? Foundation is your deliverance and support.

* * *

I do not know where this road leads. Or what it will produce. But it restores my faith that my teacher was right. Whatever decisions he may have wished to relive, if any, he placed the search first—just as I must place *capacity* before *achievement.*

This may or may not change my mind about achievement. But I know which to seek first.

Postscript: Materialism

For those unfamiliar with the historicism of what I describe, I provide a note of background.

On January 24, 1873, Karl Marx wrote in his afterword to the second German edition of *Capital, Volume I,* that Hegel grasped the "dialectic" of life but had it inverted: the movement is not driven by thoughts or ideas (or more loosely *Nous* in Hermetic terms) but rather by material and economic conditions.

As Marx saw it, Hegel's extra-physicalism had reality upside down or "standing on its head." He wrote:

> The mystification which dialectic suffers in Hegel's hands, by no means prevents him from being the first to present its general form of working in a comprehensive and conscious manner. With him it is standing on its head. It must be turned right side up again, if you would discover the rational kernel within the mystical shell. [translated by Samuel Moore and Edward Aveling]

Marx's reasoning is, I think, where the main fissure occurred between spirituality (i.e., extra-physicality) and modernism (i.e., the search for material antecedents), a division that has been over-read into the outlooks of Freud, Einstein, and Darwin.

Marx's "flipping" of Hegel into materialism is, I believe, an ur-factor in why it proves enduringly difficult for ardent materialists to accept both psi research data ("ESP has never been proven in a lab") and the unavoidably non-localist implications of quantum mechanics and computing.

As I see it, we cannot move beyond the ennui and disorientation many of us feel in a hyper-digital age unless Hegel is, so to speak, allowed to "stand on his head" as Marx found him. This is where ultimate reality dwells.

Torn from context, significant ideas are generally misunderstood, e.g., Nietzsche's "God is dead;" Crowley's "Do what thou wilt;" Fukuyama's "End of history"—and endlessly misconstrued by people (once upon a time at cocktail parties, now on social media) who have not read, and have no intention of reading, the works in which they sit. This gives a hint of what Emerson meant: "To be great is to be misunderstood" (from his—misunderstood—"Self-Reliance").

Several generations were trained on the notion of textual faithfulness—but only in those works (e.g., Marx, Freud, Marcuse) that evoked sympathies; they neglected other foundational sources, especially Hegel and the Idealists. The world just now seems adrift. But we are, I think, undergoing seismic change, almost like an under-ocean earthquake, as immaterialism is newly understood. The implications are intimate and universal.

* * *

In pursuing self-understanding, or the way out of persistent problems or conflicts, we are conditioned to seek "the answer" or a magic bullet.

We are taught to believe in an underlying key at the back of friction, self-doubt, and crisis, existential or quotidian.

This results from a formative—albeit brilliant—error in the Western psyche.

Aristotelian logic, which is responsible for the device through which you are experiencing these words, is sometimes reduced to the formula **A is A**. It is tattooed on my left forearm. I memorialize it there, in the style of Objectivist comic genius Steve Ditko (1927–2018), as a reminder to *seek ultimate causes*. This is my metaphysics.

But the formula is off. Ultimate causes are better, if less satisfyingly, represented as **A,B,C,D . . . = . . . D,C,B,A.**

Within the Aristotelian "**A is A**" framework, there exists *true* and *false*. Such logic forms the basis of binary code. And binary thinking. The either / or model is missing something: the unknown or unintelligible.

A realer representation of reality is: *true, false—and ineffable*. In endless combination.

This is represented by Yin-Yang. Its earliest written conception—yin (陰 / 阴) and yang (陽 / 阳)—dates to bone inscriptions circa 1,400 B.C. Similar soundings appear in other cultures, such as the Hermetic joining of opposites, *as above, so below*.

Due to the right / wrong, true / false, this / that imperative of Western logic—excellent for building bridges, less so for gleaning totality—we apply such absolutes to self. This habit was abetted by the modernist search for subsurface causes.

The defining principle of modernist philosophy is that life, in all its expressions, often results from unseen but knowable antecedents. This approach, in greater or lesser measure, tended toward reductionism or, in some cases, absolutism.

In politics, the modernist outlook might dictate economic clashes and inevitable cycles of revolution (Marx); in biology, evolution and natural selection (Darwin); in psychology, childhood trauma and sexual repression (Freud); in physics, time-space relativity (Einstein); in human performance, self-image (James);

in health and illness, germs and microbes (Pasteur); and so forth across myriad fields.

Bringing this to the personal, people sometimes embark on therapy or the search for self determined to discover a *root cause* to confounding problems or conflicts, whether relational, sexual, vocational, egoic, or existential.

Here we encounter a thicket: life results from a complexity of factors. I hesitate to write *causes,* as I did earlier, because even that opens the cause-correlate debate.

Because a problem or conflict or friction *results from complexity,* its resolution, acceptance, or fixing—if any exists or is needed—often, if not necessarily, results from a complexity.

* * *

I have watched seekers tangle themselves into knots due to inability to accept *paradox.*

They want a clear, clean, repeatable recipe. Everything in the endless crisscross of actuality frustrates that. We have, however, been persuaded to think otherwise. Sometimes the *otherwise* is right. Not always. Or, in the spirit of paradox, one could say it is demonstrably right and wrong.

Quantum mechanics has, for nearly a century, forced us to abide this truth in the field of scientific method and logic. In that vein, our operative parable is Schrödinger's dead / alive cat.

The error of pseudo-rationalists, i.e., those who defend strict physicalism at all costs to reality, is viewing *rationalism as outcome*. Rationalism is method. What career skeptics of the extra-physical cannot accept is: rationalism or reason *as method* places us before the ineffable. This truth will enter fuller view when quantum computing—whose performance defies all classical time-space-scale analogues—reaches public use.

What I describe is attributed to superposition. But we do not really know, outside mathematics, what superposition is. From whence do quantum solutions appear if they surpass the rules of linear time? Perhaps: other intersections of time—or dimensions.

If reality admits paradox—or superposition—at its foundations, so may our lives. Maybe what we label personal problems are not problems as such. For one thing, can there be a problem if there is no solution? Perhaps problems and solutions exist as folds of paradox: not good or bad exclusively, not this or that exclusively. They act in congruence. The answer is transmutation, *lead into gold*, rather than a fix.

Where adjustments in your life prove necessary, I say: resist nothing. Be exquisitely flexible. Adjustments, permanent or temporary, sweeping or particular, can—and almost must—arrive via multiple forms unfamiliar to the mind's eye.

Allow yourself this day to accept possibilities that stray from the accepted and repeated catalog of "ways out." The way out, if any, consists of myriad factors and unconsidered, even unwanted, channels. We have explored some in *Esoterika*.

Try them.

EPILOGUE

The Exercise

"How would you live if you knew this was your last day on earth?"

We have all heard, or repeated, some variant of this.

This familiar formulation is supposed to get us in touch with essentials. But there is a trace of self-centeredness to it. As though my personal experience is the pinnacle of life.

I once said something like this to a teacher, a senior member of the Gurdjieff work who was visiting New York City from Paris.

She reversed it on me.

"Instead of that," she said, "ask yourself, 'What if my wife and children were living their last day on earth?' What would that mean?"

To echo her: what if the people you most immediately love were living their last twenty-four hours?

For me, the search is too often public. I know the right appearances in the right settings. There is an element of theater about it.

The real search occurs out of sight. Not only in the mirror that I see—were it that simple—but in the mirror I do not see: the reflection, and results, of my acts and attitudes in the lives of others, especially those few I love. (People who love "everyone" love no one.)

I have failed in the search until that reflection is as fixed before my eyes as the reflection of my personal wants and reaches, even those I consider "inner" or "noble" or whatever self-elevating concepts I use.

I invite myself—and you—for an hour today to consider this prospect. *What if the people you most immediately love are living their last twenty-four hours?*

Can I, or you, commit an hour to that? Try.

APPENDIX

101 Rules of Effective Living

Throughout my career runs the wish to fulfill a call issued by William James during a symposium at UC Berkeley in 1898. He urged American philosophers to break with scholastic traditions of the Old World and devise philosophies of "*cash-value*, in terms of particular experience."

We have, in the short space of this book, traveled widely among different esoteric ideas and interrogations of religious tradition. It is now time, in the Jamesian sense, to cash out.

I accept and integrate into my experience only those ideals that foster honor and accountability. I revile the sneakiness endorsed in books like *The 48 Laws of Power*—if you have ever had its methods used on you, you will understand my outlook.

My spiritual philosophy is one of protean selfhood, transparency, and reciprocity. If that puts me on the losing end of the wiles race, I accept it.

Based on experience and values, the "rules" of effective, realistic, and honorable living reduce to these. I have lived, failed, tested, repeated, and fitfully succeeded with each. Success is *agency*; these are, in my best assessment, its worthiest principles.

1. Do your work—do it on time and fully, if not early and overabundantly.
2. Deal plainly.
3. Acknowledge failure.
4. There exists uncanny congruity between thought and experience.
5. Pay people on time.
6. Be willing to clean toilets and wash floors.
7. Do not over-talk.
8. Speak and write only of what you know well.
9. Apologize.
10. Judge quality not category.
11. Research every important question independently.
12. Expect corruption.
13. "Beware the devastation of conflict; war must never be pursued lightly." (Sun Tzu)
14. The loftier the language, the lower the behavior.
15. Take due credit. You will get blame when you do not deserve it.
16. Do not complain, including internally.

17. Thank people sincerely.
18. Argue with a fool—make a fool your colleague. Access confers parity.
19. Measure twice.
20. Get away from cruel people—at all costs.
21. People lie.
22. Great execution matters far more than great ideas.
23. Never humor or accommodate bullies.
24. Humiliate no one.
25. People see only those traits they possess.
26. Focus on one area of expertise and know it comprehensively.
27. Relationships define your life and happiness.
28. Never underestimate money or sex.
29. Far better to find your group than win people over.
30. When facing conflict, trust your intellect not your passions.
31. In terms of investments, virtually nothing, over time, outpaces an index fund.
32. Brilliant people are wrong all the time.
33. When you feel a sense of unease, honor it without question.
34. The only real emergency is a medical emergency.
35. Give no second chances to anyone who shows disrespect.

36. "In the long run, we find what we expect. We shall be fortunate then if we expect great things." (Thoreau)
37. Honor every religion—but: "Knowest before whom thou standeth." (Talmud, Berachot 28b)
38. Look people in the eye, recognize them, acknowledge them.
39. Tip well.
40. Eschew rhetorical questions.
41. Use sarcasm rarely.
42. Do not be an asshole.
43. Learn to fight.
44. Reduce food intake by twenty percent.
45. Better to be nobly alone than settle for low company.
46. Write nothing you would not want read aloud in public.
47. You do not know someone until witnessing him in crisis.
48. If you see someone mistreat another, he will mistreat you.
49. No one cares about your political opinions; they care only whether you agree with theirs.
50. Those who bill by the hour work not for you but for the hour.
51. "Who is evil? He who borrows and does not repay." (*Ethics of the Fathers*, Talmud)

52. Unflinching perseverance is your single best chance of deliverance. Consider this lawful.
53. Act decisively. Dithering dissipates energy and opportunity.
54. Keep your hallowed wishes private.
55. Be willing to pay qualified people for sound information or services.
56. Beware those who keep pets that bite—including people.
57. Respect workers.
58. "If we must choose between them, it is far safer to be feared than loved." (Machiavelli)
59. There is no such thing as common sense.
60. Emotions are far stronger than intellect.
61. No sincere effort is ever wasted.
62. Cynics know nothing.
63. Recheck your work—especially beginnings, endings, and "easy parts."
64. Practice constantly.
65. "To feel brave, act as if we were brave." (William James)
66. Nothing does more to squander goodwill than being a smartass.
67. Concentration produces power.
68. Test the idea by suffering it.
69. Know your preferences, even if you cannot act on them.

70. "The way bread smells depends on how hungry a man is." (Arab proverb)
71. Morality judges another; ethics judges self.
72. A positive mental attitude means evaluating circumstances based on their capacity for self-development.
73. "A chief feature of false life is that it cannot stand alone, but frantically demands allies to support its false positions." (Vernon Howard)
74. War or natural disaster abrogates nearly all of these rules; in such cases, health and survival are the laws.
75. Eschew gossip, talebearing, and trash talk—especially for entertainment.
76. Know who you are talking to.
77. Do your absolute best to carry your own load before bothering another.
78. "Opposition is true Friendship" (Blake)—but only worthy opposition.
79. Curiosity cannot be taught.
80. "Any reasonable order in an emergency is better than no order." (Major C.A. Bach)
81. "Be wise as serpents and harmless as doves." (Christ)
82. We rarely work hard enough; cease only when experiencing bodily fatigue.
83. Boredom invites trouble.

84. It is better and nobler to give away than lend money.
85. Never give up hope that your tormenter will disappear or die. It happens constantly.
86. Extra-physicality or spirituality is as real as the words you are now reading.
87. There is no dishonor in electing to give in. Conflicts must end.
88. "He who proceeds violently across the earth will meet with a weary end. Know this and you know all my teachings." (Lao Tzu)
89. Arrogance is stupidity.
90. Never pick on people or make jokes at their expense; they have more problems than you know.
91. Know whether you are guest or host and the obligations of each.
92. The only things you can really give another are money or time.
93. "Persistence amounting to madness should be avoided." (I Ching, hexagram 36)
94. Accept paradox.
95. "Chance favors the prepared mind." (Pasteur)
96. Steel yourself for the day when your best friend betrays you.
97. Keep your word.
98. No one is as confident as he who knows the least.

99. Show respect.
100. Do not rephrase ideas you have not lived with.
101. Ask constantly: how do I know that's true?

To this I add a postscript: Do not grow fascinated with people who dislike you. It is a universal of human nature that we project our insecurities onto what we cannot have, including relationships and approval, hence elevating their perceived value.

Index

Note: Page numbers followed by "n" indicate material in notes.

About the Author

Portrait by Sante D'Orazio

Mitch Horowitz is a PEN Award-winning historian, writer, and lecturer who explores the intersections of metaphysics, ethics, and self-transformation. His books include *Occult America, The Miracle Club, Modern Occultism, Daydream Believer,* and *Practical Magick*. Mitch is featured in Critics' Choice-nominated and Sundance-premiering films, as well as numerous television shows. David Lynch: "Mitch is solid gold."

About the Cover

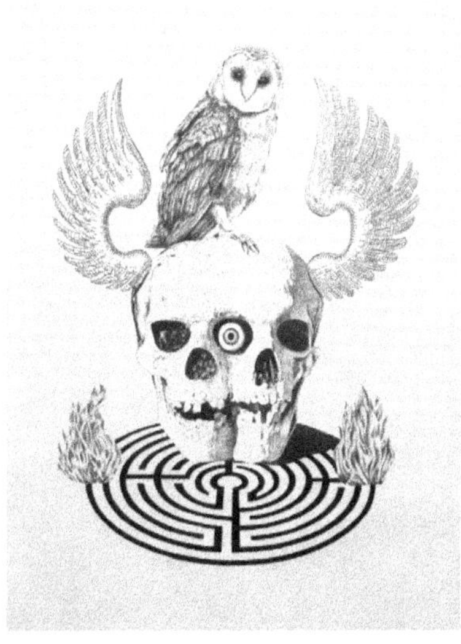

John Newsom
Esoterika, 2026
Pencil on paper
60 x 44 inches

The cover by fine artist **John Newsom** shows the reconciling wisdom of the search: the owl—both predator (protector) and seer in the dark—perched atop the active and passive efforts of temporal life, themselves situated on a labyrinth of seeking amid the twin flames and wings of effort. The owl anoints the unified eye of vision: knowing of self; being and intention joined within the concentric circles of existence. John did not know this when I asked him to create the cover, but my teacher—quoted many times in *Esoterika*—was deemed an owl by one of his.

www.ingramcontent.com/pod-product-compliance
Lightning Source LLC
Chambersburg PA
CBHW071534030726
47598CB00001B/133

9781722507626